KETO SOUP AND **STEWS** 2019-2020

Delicious,Easy, Fat Burning Soup &
Stews for Busy people on Keto Diet

DR. MARIA ELLIOTT

TABLE OF CONTENTS

DESCRIPTION

There is no better way of warming up and preparing for a delicious meal than having a tasty keto soup. They are easy to make, yet healthy, and you yearn to take more each day. Ketosoups and rich in fat and low in carbs, thus aiding a faster weight loss. With the ketogenic diet, your fat loss happens quickly and in a healthy manner because your body is using your fat reserves for energy even while doing your mundane tasks. You don't feel hungry on this diet. Your body turns itself into a fat burning machine.

This is an amazing guide with tasty, finger licking soups. What are you waiting for? Grab this copy and start enjoying this delicious homemade soups for a happy day and a healthy you!

INTRODUCTION

Eating on the keto diet requires a bit of planning, discipline, and adjustments. Since, you will no longer be feeding heavily on carbs, what then serves as replacements for the carb take-outs? Below I share a long list of things to exclude from the diet and then the foods to enjoy.

To achieve success will require a bit of planning around your eating patterns, food supply, budget, and schedules to ensure that your daily macro requirements are consistently on point. If you're having aches and suffering from inflammation...

Sugar is inflammatory, and because ketosis uses fat instead of sugar for energy, a keto diet can be a big help in dealing with inflammation. Ketogenic foods help in reducing inflammation, according to experts. Foods from a keto diet plan can cease the surges of insulin due to unregulated levels of sugar. When there is an increase of sugar level in the body, this will lead to inflammation.

KETO SOUPS RECIPES

01. Cheesy Cauliflower Soup

Servings: 3

Ingredients:

- 2 cups chicken broth
- 1 small head cauliflower, chopped
- 1 clove minced garlic
- ½ cup heavy cream
- ½ cup shredded cheddar cheese
- Salt and pepper

Directions:

1. Warm the chicken broth in a medium saucepan over medium heat.
2. Add the cauliflower and garlic then bring to a boil.
3. Reduce heat and simmer for 15 minutes until the cauliflower is tender
4. Stir in the cream and cheese then season with salt and pepper.
5. Blend or use an immersion blender to puree and serve hot.

Nutrition Value: 195 calories, 15g fat, 10g protein, 6.5g carbs, 2g fiber, 4.5g net carbs

02. Pumpkin Ginger Soup

Servings: 3

Ingredients:

- 1 cup fresh pumpkin
- 1 tablespoon olive oil

- ½ small yellow onion, chopped
- 1 clove minced garlic
- 1 tablespoon grated ginger
- 2 cups chicken broth

Directions:

1. Bring a pot of salted water to boil then add the fresh pumpkin.
2. Boil until the pumpkin is soften then drain and mash it well.
3. Heat the oil in a saucepan over medium heat.
4. Add the onion, garlic, and ginger then cook for 3 minutes, stirring.
5. Add the pumpkin then cook for 2 minutes.
6. Stir in the chicken broth then bring to a boil.
7. Reduce heat and simmer for 20 minutes then remove from heat.
8. Puree the soup using an immersion blender then adjust seasoning to taste.

Nutrition Value: 60 calories, 9g fat, 7g protein, 15g carbs, 5g fiber, 10g net carbs

03. Broccoli Cheddar Soup

Servings: 4

Ingredients:

- 1 tablespoon butter
- ½ small white onion, diced
- 1 cup chopped broccoli
- 2 cups chicken broth
- ¼ cup heavy cream
- 1 cup shredded cheddar cheese

Directions:

1. Sauté the onion in butter in a saucepan over medium heat until the onions are translucent.
2. Stir in the broccoli and chicken broth then bring to a boil.
3. Reduce heat and simmer until the broccoli is tender, about 10 to 12 minutes.
4. Stir in the cream then season with salt and pepper.
5. Remove from heat then stir in the cheddar cheese. Serve hot.

Nutrition Value: 200 calories, 16g fat, 10.5g protein, 3.5g carbs, 1g fiber, 2.5g net carbs

04. Buffalo Chicken Soup

Servings: 4

Ingredients:
- 2 tablespoons butter
- ½ small yellow onion, chopped
- 2 cups half-n-half
- 1 cup chopped chicken breast
- 2 tablespoons hot sauce
- 1 cup shredded cheddar cheese

Directions:
1. Heat the butter in a saucepan on medium-high heat.
2. Add the onion and sauté until tender then stir in the flour.
3. Cook for another 2 minutes then add the half-and-half.
4. Stir in the chicken, hot sauce, and cheddar cheese then season with salt and pepper.
5. Reduce heat and simmer on medium-low until the cheese is melted, about 10 minutes.

Nutrition Value: 355 calories, 30g fat, 16g protein, 6.5g carbs. 0.5g fiber, 6g net carbs

05. Cucumber Avocado Soup

Servings: 3

Ingredients:
- 1 medium seedless cucumber, peeled and chopped
- 1 small avocado, chopped
- ¼ cup fresh cilantro
- 2 tablespoons apple cider vinegar
- 1 clove minced garlic
- ¾ cup water

Directions:
1. Combine the cucumber, avocado, cilantro, vinegar, and garlic in a blender and blend until smooth and well combined.
2. Add up to 1 cup of water, a little at a time, until thinned to the desired texture.
3. Season with salt and pepper then chill until ready to serve.

Nutrition Value: 150 calories, 13g fat, 2g protein, 7.5g carbs, 5g fiber, 2.5g net carbs

06. Mexican Chicken Soup

Servings: 2

Ingredients:
- ½ pound boneless chicken thighs
- ½ cup diced tomatoes
- ½ small yellow onion, chopped
- 2 cloves minced garlic
- 1 cup chicken broth
- ½ cup shredded cheddar cheese

Directions:

1. Combine the chicken, tomatoes, onion, and garlic in a slow cooker.
2. Pour in the chicken broth then season with salt and pepper.
3. Cover and cook on high heat for 2 to 3 hours then shred the chicken.
4. Stir in the cheddar cheese and cook for another 20 minutes.
5. Serve hot topped with sour cream and diced avocado.

Nutrition Value:: 400 calories, 27g fat, 30g protein, 5g carbs, 1g fiber, 4g net carbs

07. Thick Chicken Breast Soup with Herbs

Servings: 6
Preparation Time: 10 minutes
Cooking Time: 8 hours

Ingredients

- 1 green onion finely sliced
- 1 lb of chicken breast, boneless
- 1 grated tomato
- 1 tsp of dry coriander
- 1 tsp of red ground paprika
- 1 tsp of fresh ginger, grated
- Salt and ground pepper to taste
- 2 tsp of turmeric
- 4 tsp of ground cinnamon
- 2 tsp of garlic powder
- 1 cup water
- 3 Tbsp of almond flour
- 2 Tbsp of cold water

Directions

1. Season chicken breast with the salt and pepper and place in your Crock Pot.
2. In a medium-sized bowl, combine tomatoes, coriander, paprika, ginger, turmeric, cinnamon and garlic powder; add water, stir and pour in Crock Pot.
3. Cover and cook on LOW for 8 hours or at HIGH for 4-5 hours.
4. In a small bowl, dilute the almond flour in water and pour the mixture into Crock Pot
5. Cover again and cook on HIGH for further 15-20 minutes or until thickened.
6. Adjust salt, stir and serve hot.

Nutrition Value: Calories: 30 Carbs: 3.5g Proteins: 3g Fat: 1g Fiber: 4g

08. Green Beans Power Soup

Servings: 6
Preparation Time: 5 minutes
Cooking Time: 8 hours

Ingredients

*   2 lbs green beans - trimmed and cut diagonally in half
*   1 small onion, diced
*   1 clove garlic, minced
*   1 carrot, sliced
*   2 Tbsp fresh cilantro, chopped
*   2 cups bone broth (preferable homemade)
*   2 cups water
*   1 tsp chili powder
*   1 tsp cumin
*   Salt and ground pepper to taste

Directions

1. Place all ingredients in the Slow Cooker, and stir well.
2. Cover and cook on LOW for 6-8 hours.
3. Taste and adjust seasonings.
4. Serve hot.

Nutrition Value: Calories: 65 Carbs: 4g Proteins: 6g Fat: 1g Fiber: 0.2g

09. Keto Kimchi Soup

Servings: 6
Preparation Time: 10 minutes
Cooking Time: 3 hours

Ingredients

- 2 lb of fresh pork belly
- Sea salt and black pepper or to taste
- 4 lb of Napa cabbage, chopped
- 2 cup of spring onions finely chopped
- 4 cup of fresh button mushrooms
- 1 tsp of stevia sweetener
- 1 tsp ground paprika
- 2 Tbsp of coconut aminos
- 3 Tbsp of sesame oil
- 4 cups of water

Directions

1. Cut pork belly into pieces and season with the salt and pepper.
2. Place meat in Slow Cooker and add chopped Napa cabbage, spring onions and mushrooms.
3. In a small bowl, stir water, sesame oil, stevia, ground paprika and coconut aminos.
4. Pour mixture in your Slow Cooker over meat and vegetables.

5. Cover and cook on HIGH for 3 hours.
6. Taste and adjust seasonings.
7. Serve.

Nutrition Value: Calories: 110 Carbs: 2g Proteins: 1g Fat: 12g Fiber: 0.4g

10. Weight-Loss Broccoli Cream Soup

Servings: 4
Preparation Time: 10 minutes
Cooking Time: 20 minutes

Ingredients
- 1 lb broccoli
- 2 green onions, finely chopped
- 2 stalks celery white
- 1 cup cauliflower floweret
- 3 Tbsp olive oil
- 2 cup water
- 2 tsp garlic powder
- Salt and pepper to taste

Directions
1. In a deep pan heat the oil, and sauté the green onion and chopped celery.
2. Add in the broccoli and cauliflower.
3. Season the salt and pepper to taste, and add the garlic powder.
4. Pour water into pot, stir and cook for 15 - 20 minutes.
5. When ready, pour the soup into blender and bit to a very fine cream.
6. Serve.

Nutrition Value: Calories: 164 Carbs: 8g Proteins: 5g Fat: 17g Fiber: 1.5g

11. Wild Mushrooms Soup with Eggs

Servings: 4
Preparation Time: 5 minutes
Cooking Time: 20 minutes

Ingredients

- 2 Tbsp of extra-virgin olive oil
- 1 lb wild mushrooms (chanterelles or porcini)
- 1 scallion, finely chopped
- 2 garlic clove, finely chopped
- 2 cups bone broth (preferable homemade)
- 2 cups water
- 2 egg yolks from free-range chicken
- 2 Tbsp of lemon juice
- Salt and freshly ground pepper to taste

Directions

1. Heat the oil in a pot over medium-high heat.
2. Add mushrooms and stir for 3 minutes; season the salt and pepper.
3. Reduce the heat to medium, add the scallion and garlic, and cook for 3 minutes.
4. Pour the bone broth and water, stir, cover and cook for 10 - 12 minutes.
5. In a bowl, whisk egg yolks with a pinch of salt and lemon juice.
6. Pour the egg mixture in a pot, turn off heat, and stir for further 2 - 3 minutes.
7. Taste and adjust the salt and pepper to taste. Serve hot.

Nutrition Value: Calories: 130 Carbs: 2g Proteins: 18g Fat: 13g Fiber: 0.3g

12. Winter Cabbage and Celery Soup

Servings: 6
Preparation Time: 5 minutes
Cooking Time: 30 minutes

Ingredients

- 2 Tbsp olive oil
- 2 cloves garlic, minced
- 2 head cabbage, shredded
- 2 stalks celery, chopped
- 1 grated tomato
- 3 cups bone broth (preferable homemade)
- 3 cups water
- 2 tsp ground black pepper

Directions

1. Heat the oil in a large pot over medium heat.
2. Sauté the garlic, celery and cabbage, stirring, for about 8 minutes.
3. Add grated tomato, and continue to cook for further 2 - 3 minutes.
4. Pour the broth and water. Bring to a boil, lower heat to low, cover and simmer for 20 minutes or until cabbage softened.
5. Sprinkle with ground black pepper, stir and serve.

Nutrition Value: Calories: 85 Carbs: 2g Proteins: 17g Fat: 11g Fiber: 1g

13. Spinach Soup with Shiitake mushrooms

Servings: 4
Preparation Time: 10 minutes
Cooking Time: 15 minutes

Ingredients

- 2 Tbsp of olive oil

- 1 medium onion, chopped
- 2 cloves garlic, minced
- 2 cups of water
- 2 bunch of spinach
- 2 cups shiitake mushrooms, chopped
- 2 Tbsp of almond flour
- 1 Tbsp of coconut aminos
- 1 tsp coriander dry
- 2 tsp of ground mustard
- Salt and ground black pepper to taste

Directions

1. Heat the olive oil and sauté the garlic and onion until golden brown.
2. Add the coconut aminos and the mushrooms and stir for a few minutes.
3. Pour water, chopped spinach and all remaining ingredients.
4. Cover and cook for 5 - 6 minutes or until spinach is tender.
5. Taste and adjust salt and the pepper.
6. Stir for further 5 minutes and remove for the heat.
7. Serve hot.

Nutrition Value: Calories: 175 Carbs: 12g Proteins: 21g Fat: 8g Fiber: 4.3g

14. Vegan Artichoke Soup

Servings: 6
Preparation Time: 15 minutes
Cooking Time: 1 hour 5 minutes

Ingredients

- 1 Tbsp of butter

- 6 artichoke hearts, halved
- 2 cloves garlic, minced
- 1 small onion, chopped
- 1 cup bone broth
- 2 cups of water
- 2 Tbsp of almond flour
- Salt and ground black pepper to taste
- 2 Tbsp of olive oil
- Fresh chopped parsley to taste
- Fresh chopped fresh basil to taste

Directions
1. Heat the butter in a large pot, and add artichoke hearts, garlic and chopped onion.
2. Stir and cook until artichoke hearts tender.
3. Add bone broth, water and almond flout: season with the salt and pepper.
4. Bring soup to boil, and cook for 2 minutes.
5. Add little olive oil, parsley and basil, stir and cook uncovered for 1 hour.
6. When ready, push the soup through sieve.
7. Taste and adjust salt and pepper.
8. Serve.

Nutrition Value: Calories: 145 Carbs: 6g Proteins: 7g Fat: 12g Fiber: 0.5%

15. Bouyambessa" Seafood Soup

Servings: 6
Preparation Time: 10 minutes
Cooking Time: 25 minutes

Ingredients
- 2 cup of olive oil

- 1 spring onion cut in cubes
- 2 Tbsp of fresh celery, chopped
- 2 cloves of garlic minced
- 1 tomato, peeled and grated
- 2 bay leaves
- 1 tsp of anise
- 6 large, raw shrimps
- 1 sea bass and 1 sea bream fillets cut in pieces; about 1 1
- 2 lbs
- 12 mussels, rinsed in plenty of cold water
- Salt and ground black pepper
- 3 Tbsp of chopped parsley for serving
- 6 cups of water

Directions

1. Heat the olive oil in a large pot and sauté in the onion, garlic and celery for 4 -5 minutes over medium heat.
2. Add bay leaves, anise and grated tomato; stir and cook for further 5 minutes.
3. Add seafood and fish and pour 6 cups of water; season with little salt and pepper.
4. Cover and cook for 10 - 12 minutes on low heat. Serve hot with chopped parsley.

Nutrition Value: Calories: 272.5 Carbs: 2g Proteins: 19g Fat: 20g Fiber: 0.5g

16. Classico" Beef Stew

Servings: 8
Preparation Time: 5 minutes
Cooking Time: 1 hour 35 minutes

Ingredients

2 lb beef filed, cut in cubes

1 green onion (white and green parts), chopped

- 2 cloves garlic, minced
- 1 small carrot
- 1 grated tomato
- 1 tsp fresh basil (chopped)
- 1 tsp fresh oregano chopped
- 3 cups bone broth (or water)
- 2 cup white vinegar
- 1 tsp salt
- 1 Tbsp lard

Directions

1. Heat the lard in a large skillet and sauté beef meat with a pinch of salt.
2. Add the onion and garlic, and cook until soft.
3. Add grated tomato and the carrot and stir for further 2 minutes.
4. Add all the other ingredients cover and cook on very low heat for about 1 1
5. 2 to 1 3
6. 4 hours, until the beef is tender.
7. Serve hot.

Nutrition Value: Calories: 498 Carbs: 3g Proteins: 46g Fat: 42g Fiber: 1g

17. Chicken and Greens Soup

Servings: 8

Preparation Time: 12 minutes

Cooking Time: 1 hour 50 minutes

Ingredients

- 4 cup of olive oil

- 2 lbs chicken breast, boneless, cut into cube
- 1 spring onion, cut into cubes
- 1 clove of garlic, finely chopped
- 2 lettuce cos or romain, chopped
- 1 cup of fresh spinach finely chopped
- 1 bunch of dill finely chopped, without the thick stalks
- 2 Tbsp of sweet chill powder
- 1 tsp of fresh mint, chopped
- 1 tsp of fresh thyme, chopped
- Salt and freshly ground pepper
- 5 cups of water

Directions

1. In a deep pot, heat the olive oil to a high heat and sauté the chicken for about 5 - 6 minutes.
2. Add the onion and sauté for about 3 minutes until softened.
3. Add the garlic, the lettuce, spinach, dill, mint, thyme and sauté for about 3-4 minutes, stirring with a wooden spoon.
4. Sprinkle with chili, salt, freshly ground pepper and pour 5 cups of water.
5. Bring to boil, and cook for 1 1
6. 2 hours on low heat.
7. Serve hot.

Nutrition Value: Calories: 181 Carbs: 4.5g Proteins: 20g Fat: 10g Fiber: 3g

18. Cold Cauliflower and Cilantro Soup

Servings: 4
Preparation Time: 5 minutes
Cooking Time: 25 minutes

Ingredients

- 2 lbs. cauliflower (previously steamed)
- 1 cup almond milk
- 2 tsp fresh ginger grated
- 3 bunches fresh cilantro
- 3 Tbsp garlic-infused olive oil
- 2 pinch of salt

Directions

1. Heat water in a large pot until boiling. Place the steamer in a pot and put in the cauliflower.
2. Cover and steam cauliflower for 6 - 7 minutes.
3. Remove the cauliflower along with all ingredients from the list above in a high-speed blender.
4. Blend until smooth or until desired texture is achieved.
5. Pour the soup in a glass container, cover and refrigerate for 2 - 3 hours.
6. Serve cold.

Nutrition Value: Calories: 132 Carbs: 7.5g Proteins: 3.5g Fat: 11g Fiber: 3.5g

19. Creamy Broccoli Soup with Nutmeg

Servings: 6
Preparation Time: 15 minutes
Cooking Time: 20 minutes

Ingredients

- 2 Tbsp of olive oil
- 2 green onions finely chopped
- 1 lb broccoli floret, frozen or fresh
- 6 cups of bone broth (cold)
- 1 cup of cream
- Salt and ground pepper to taste

- 1 Tbsp of nutmeg

Directions

1. Heat the olive oil in a pot over medium-high heat.
2. Add the onion in and sauté it until becomes translucent.
3. Add the broccoli, season with the salt and pepper, and bring to boil.
4. Cover the pot and cook for 6 - 8 minutes.
5. Transfer the broccoli mixture into blender, and blend until smooth.
6. Pour the cream, and blend for further 30 seconds.
7. Return the soup in a pot, and reheat it.
8. Adjust salt and pepper, and serve hot with grated nutmeg.

Nutrition Value:

Calories: 205 Carbs: 5g Proteins: 35g Fat: 18g Fiber: 0.4g

20. Creamy Mushroom Soup with Crumbled Bacon

Servings: 6
Preparation Time: 15 minutes
Cooking Time: 55 minutes

Ingredients

- 1 Tbsp of lard
- 2 lbs of white mushrooms
- 2 cup of water
- 2 cups of almond milk
- 2 green onions, finely sliced
- 3 sprigs of fresh rosemary
- 2 cloves garlic, finely chopped
- 6 slices of bacon, fried and crumbled
- Salt and ground black pepper

Directions

1. Heat the lard in a large skillet and sauté green onions and garlic over medium-high heat.
2. Season with the salt and pepper, and rosemary; pour water and cook for 5 minutes.
3. Add the mushrooms and sauté for 1-2 minutes.
4. Pour the almond milk, stir, cover and simmer for 40 minutes over low heat.
5. Remove the rosemary, and transfer the soup in your blender; blend until creamy and soft.
6. Adjust salt, and if necessary, add some warm water.
7. Chop the bacon and fry in a hot pan until it becomes crisp.
8. Serve your soup in bowls and sprinkle with chopped bacon.

Nutrition Value: Calories: 101 Carbs: 5.5g Proteins: 8g Fat: 6g Fiber: 2g

21. Fragrant "Greenery" Soup

Servings: 6
Preparation Time: 10 minutes
Cooking Time: 25 minutes

Ingredients

- 3 cup olive oil
- 1 leek, the white and tender green part, cut into slices
- 2 fresh onions, white and tender green part, finely chopped
- 1 lb of various greens (spinach, lettuce, chard, etc.), coarsely chopped
- Salt and ground pepper to taste
- 4 tsp of nutmeg
- 6 cups of water
- 2 cup of fresh dill, finely chopped

Directions

1. Pout the oil in a pot, and sauté the leek, fresh onions and greens for 5 minutes; stir.
2. Season with the salt and pepper, grated nutmeg and pour water; bring to boil.
3. Cover and cook for 8 - 10 minutes over medium-low heat.
4. When the vegetables softened, transfer them in a blender; blend until soft.
5. Serve in a bowl, and sprinkle each serving with fresh dill and freshly ground pepper.

Nutrition Value: Calories: 140 Carbs: 6g Proteins: 4g Fat: 13g Fiber: 1g

22. Avocado Soup

Preparation time: 10 minutes
Cooking time: 10 minutes
Servings: 4

Ingredients:

- 2 avocados, pitted, peeled, and chopped
- 3 cups chicken stock
- 2 scallions, chopped
- Salt and ground black pepper, to taste
- 2 tablespoons butter
- ⅔ cup heavy cream

Directions:

1. Heat a saucepan with butter over medium heat, add scallions, stir, and cook for 2 minutes.
2. Add 2½ cups stock, stir, and simmer for 3 minutes.
3. In a blender, mix avocados with rest of the stock, salt, pepper, heavy cream, and pulse well. Add to the pan, stir well, cook for 2 minutes, and season with more

salt and pepper.
4. Stir, ladle into soup bowls, and serve.

Nutrition Value: Calories: 335, Fat: 33.2, Fiber: 6.9, Carbs: 10.3, Protein: 3

23. Avocado and Bacon Soup

Preparation time: 10 minutes
Cooking time: 10 minutes
Servings: 4

Ingredients:
- 2 avocados, pitted, and cut in half
- 4 cups chicken stock
- ⅓ cup fresh cilantro, chopped
- Juice of ½ lime
- 1 teaspoon garlic powder
- ½ pound bacon, cooked, and chopped
- Salt and ground black pepper, to taste

Directions:
1. Put the stock in a saucepan and bring to a boil over medium–high heat.
2. In a blender, mix avocados with garlic powder, cilantro, lime juice, salt, pepper, and blend well. Add to the stock and blend using an immersion blender.
3. Add bacon, more salt and pepper, stir, cook for 3 minutes, ladle into soup bowls, and serve.

Nutrition Value: Calories: 524, Fat: 43.9, Fiber: 6.8, Carbs: 10.7, Protein: 23.7

24. Thai Avocado Soup

Preparation time: 10 minutes
Cooking time: 10 minutes

Servings: 4

Ingredients:
- 1 cup coconut milk
- 2 teaspoons Thai green curry paste
- 1 avocado, pitted, peeled, and chopped
- 1 tablespoon fresh cilantro, chopped
- Salt and ground black pepper, to taste
- 2 cups vegetable stock
- Lime wedges, for serving

Directions:
1. In a blender, mix avocado with salt, pepper, curry paste, coconut milk, and pulse well.
2. Transfer to a saucepan and heat over medium heat.
3. Add stock, stir, bring to a simmer, and cook for 5 minutes.
4. Add cilantro, more salt and pepper, stir, cook for 1 minute, ladle into soup bowls, and serve with lime wedges.

Nutrition Value: Calories: 250, Fat: 24.9, Fiber: 5, Carbs: 8.2, Protein: 2.4

25. Arugula Soup

Preparation time: 10 minutes
Cooking time: 13 minutes
Servings: 6

Ingredients:
- 1 onion, peeled and chopped
- 1 tablespoon olive oil
- 2 garlic cloves, peeled and minced
- ½ cup coconut milk
- 10 ounces baby arugula

- 2 tablespoons fresh mint, chopped, and
- 2 tablespoons fresh tarragon, chopped
- 2 tablespoons fresh parsley, chopped
- 2 tablespoons fresh chives, chopped
- 4 tablespoons coconut milk yogurt
- 6 cups chicken stock
- Salt and ground black pepper, to taste

Directions:

1. Heat a saucepan with oil over medium–high heat, add onion and garlic, stir, and cook for 5 minutes.
2. Add stock, milk, stir, and bring to a simmer.
3. Add arugula, tarragon, parsley, mint, stir, and cook for 6 minutes.
4. Add coconut yogurt, salt, pepper, chives, stir, cook for 2 minutes, divide into soup bowls, and serve.

Nutrition Value:: Calories: 186, Fat: 11.4, Fiber: 7.9, Carbs: 20.9, Protein: 4.2

26. Arugula and Broccoli Soup

Preparation time: 10 minutes
Cooking time: 20 minutes
Servings: 4

Ingredients:

- 1 onion, peeled and chopped
- 1 tablespoon olive oil
- 1 garlic clove, peeled and minced
- 1 broccoli head, separated into florets
- Salt and ground black pepper, to taste
- 2, and ½ cups vegetable stock
- 1 teaspoon cumin
- Juice of ½ lemon

- 1 cup arugula leaves

Directions:
1. Heat a saucepan with the over medium–high heat, add onions, stir, and cook for 4 minutes.
2. Add garlic, stir, and cook for 1 minute.
3. Add broccoli, cumin, salt, and pepper, stir, and cook for 4 minutes. Add stock, stir, and cook for 8 minutes.
4. Blend soup using an immersion blender, add half of arugula, and blend again.
5. Add rest of the arugula, stir, and heat up soup again.
6. Add lemon juice, stir, ladle into soup bowls, and serve.

Nutrition Value: Calories: 74, Fat: 4.9, Fiber: 2.5, Carbs: 8.8, Protein: 2.5

27. Zucchini Cream

Preparation time: 10 minutes
Cooking time: 25 minutes
Servings: 8

Ingredients:
- 6 zucchini, cut in half and sliced
- Salt and ground black pepper, to taste
- 1 tablespoon butter
- 28 ounces vegetable stock
- 1 teaspoon dried oregano
- ½ cup onion, chopped
- 3 garlic cloves, peeled and minced
- 2 ounces Parmesan cheese, grated
- ¾ cup heavy cream

Directions:
1. Heat a saucepan with the butter over medium–high heat, add onion, stir, and cook for 4 minutes.

2. Add garlic, stir, and cook for 2 minutes.
3. Add zucchini, stir, and cook for 3 minutes.
4. Add stock, stir, bring to a boil, and simmer over medium heat for 15 minutes.
5. Add oregano, salt, pepper, stir, take off heat, and blend using an immersion blender.
6. Heat soup again, add heavy cream, stir, and bring to a simmer.
7. Add Parmesan cheese, stir, take off heat, ladle into bowls, and serve.

Nutrition Value: Calories: 109, Fat: 7.5, Fiber: 2.4, Carbs: 7.5, Protein: 4.9

28. Zucchini and Avocado Soup

Preparation time: 10 minutes
Cooking time: 15 minutes
Servings: 4

Ingredients:
- 1 big avocado, pitted, peeled, and chopped
- 4 scallions, chopped
- 1 teaspoon fresh ginger, grated
- 2 tablespoons avocado oil
- Salt and ground black pepper, to taste
- 2 zucchini, chopped
- 29 ounces vegetable stock
- 1 garlic clove, peeled and minced
- 1 cup water
- 1 tablespoon lemon juice
- 1 red bell pepper, seeded and chopped

Directions:
1. Heat a saucepan with the over medium heat, add onions, stir, and cook for 3 minutes.

2. Add garlic and ginger, stir, and cook for 1 minute.
3. Add zucchini, salt, pepper, water, stock, stir, bring to a boil, cover the pan, and cook for 10 minutes.
4. Take off heat, set soup aside for a couple of minutes, add avocado, stir, blend everything using an immersion blender, and heat up again.
5. Add more salt and pepper, plus the bell pepper and lemon juice, stir, heat up soup again, ladle into soup bowls, and serve.

Nutrition Value:: Calories: 155, Fat: 11.1, Fiber: 6.4, Carbs: 13.5, Protein: 3.7

29. Power Green Soup

Preparation Time: 30 minutes
Servings: 6

Ingredients
- 1 broccoli head, chopped
- 1 cup spinach
- 1 onion, chopped
- 2 garlic cloves, minced
- ½ cup watercress
- 5 cups veggie stock
- 1 cup coconut milk
- 1 tsp salt
- 1 tbsp ghee
- 1 bay leaf
- Salt and black pepper, to taste

Directions
1. Melt the ghee in a large pot over medium heat. Add onion and cook for 3 minutes. Add garlic and cook for another minute. Add broccoli and cook for an additional 5 minutes.

2. Pour the stock over and add the bay leaf. Close the lid, bring to a boil, and reduce the heat. Simmer for about 3 minutes.
3. In the end, add spinach and watercress, and cook for 3 more minutes. Stir in the coconut cream, salt and pepper. Discard the bay leaf, and blend the soup with a hand blender.

Nutrition Value: Calories 392, Fat: 37.6g, Net Carbs: 5.8g, Protein: 4.9g

30. Beef Reuben Soup

Preparation Time: 20 minutes
Servings: 6

Ingredients

- 1 onion, diced
- 6 cups beef stock
- 1 tsp caraway seeds
- 2 celery stalks, diced
- 2 garlic cloves, minced
- ¾ tsp black pepper
- 2 cups heavy cream
- 1 cup sauerkraut
- 1 pound corned beef, chopped
- 3 tbsp butter
- 1 ½ cup swiss cheese
- Salt and black pepper, to taste

Directions

1. Melt the butter in a large pot. Add onion and celery, and fry for 3 minutes until tender. Add garlic and cook for another minute.
2. Pour the broth over and stir in sauerkraut, salt, caraway seeds, and add a pinch of pepper. Bring to a

boil. Reduce the heat to low, and add the corned beef. Cook for about 15 minutes, adjust the seasoning. Stir in heavy cream and cheese and cook for 1 minute.

Nutrition Value: Calories 450, Fat: 37g, Net Carbs: 8g, Protein: 23g

31. Chicken Creamy Soup

Preparation Time: 15 minutes
Servings: 4

Ingredients

- 2 cups cooked and shredded chicken
- 3 tbsp butter, melted
- 4 cups chicken broth
- 4 tbsp chopped cilantro
- ⅓ cup buffalo sauce
- ½ cup cream cheese
- Salt and black pepper, to taste

Directions

1. Blend the butter, buffalo sauce, and cream cheese, in a food processor, until smooth. Transfer to a pot, add the chicken broth and heat until hot but do not bring to a boil. Stir in chicken and cook until heated through. When ready, remove to soup bowls and serve garnished with cilantro.

Nutrition Value: Calories 406, Fat: 29.5g, Net Carbs: 5g, Protein: 26.5g

32. Salsa Verde Chicken Soup

Preparation Time: 15 minutes
Servings: 4

Ingredients

- ½ cup salsa verde
- 2 cups cooked and shredded chicken
- 2 cups chicken broth
- 1 cup shredded cheddar cheese
- 4 ounces cream cheese
- ½ tsp chili powder
- ½ tsp ground cumin
- ½ tsp fresh cilantro, chopped
- Salt and black pepper, to taste

Directions

2. Combine the cream cheese, salsa verde, and broth, in a food processor; pulse until smooth. Transfer the mixture to a pot and place over medium heat. Cook until hot, but do not bring to a boil.
3. Add chicken, chili powder, and cumin and cook for about 3-5 minutes, or until it is heated through.
4. Stir in Cheddar cheese and season with salt and pepper to taste. If it is very thick, add a few tablespoons of water and boil for 1-3 more minutes. Serve hot in bowls sprinkled with fresh cilantro.

Nutrition Value: Calories 346, Fat: 23g, Net Carbs: 3g, Protein: 25g

33. Broccoli Cheese Soup

Preparation Time:20 minutes
Servings: 4

Ingredients

- ¾ cup heavy cream
- 1 onion, diced
- 1 tsp minced garlic
- 4 cups chopped broccoli
- 4 cups veggie broth

- 2 tbsp butter
- 2 ¾ cups grated cheddar cheese
- ¼ cup cheddar cheese to garnish
- Salt and black pepper, to taste
- ½ bunch fresh mint, chopped

Directions

1. Melt the butter in a large pot over medium heat. Sauté onion and garlic for 3 minutes or until tender, stirring occasionally. Season with salt and pepper. Add the broth, broccoli and bring to a boil.

2. Reduce the heat and simmer for 10 minutes. Puree the soup with a hand blender until smooth. Add in the cheese and cook about 1 minute. Taste, season with salt and pepper. Stir in the heavy cream.Serve in bowls with the reserved grated Cheddar cheese and sprinkled with fresh mint.

Nutrition Value: Calories 561, Fat: 52.3g, Net Carbs: 7g, Protein: 23.8g

34. Monterey Jack Cheese Soup

Preparation Time: 20 minutes
Servings: 4

Ingredients

- 2 tbsp butter
- ½ cup leeks, chopped
- 1 celery stalk, chopped
- 1 serrano pepper, finely chopped
- 1 tsp garlic puree
- 1 ½ tbsp flax seed meal
- 2 cups water
- 1 ½ cups coconut milk
- 6 ounces Monterey Jack cheese, shredded

- Salt and black pepper, to taste
- Fresh parsley, chopped to garnish

Directions

1. Set a deep pan over medium heat and melt butter. Add in serrano pepper, celery and leeks and sauté until soft. Place in coconut milk, garlic paste, water, and flaxseed meal.
2. While covered partially, allow simmering for 10 minutes or until cooked through.
3. Fold in the shredded cheese, kill the heat and stir to ensure the cheese is completely melted and you have a homogenous mixture. Add pepper and salt for seasoning to taste.
4. Divide among serving bowls, decorate with parsley and serve while warm.

Nutrition Value: Calories 296; Fat 14.1g, Net Carbs 7.4g, Protein 14.2g

35. Asian Tofu Egg Soup

Preparation Time: 15 minutes
Servings: 3

Ingredients

- 3 cups chicken stock
- 1 tbsp tamari sauce
- 1 tsp coconut oil, softened
- 2 eggs, beaten
- ½ tsp turmeric powder
- 1-inch piece ginger, grated
- Salt and black ground, to taste
- ¼ tsp paprika
- ½ pound extra-firm tofu, cubed
- A handful of fresh cilantro, chopped

Directions

1. Set a pan over medium heat, add in tamari sauce, stock, and coconut oil; allow boiling. Place in eggs as you whisk to incorporate completely. Change heat to low and add turmeric, salt, paprika, black pepper and ginger. Place in tofu and simmer for 1 to 2 minutes.
2. Divide into soup bowls and serve sprinkled with fresh cilantro.

Nutrition Value: Calories 153; Fat: 9.8g, Net Carbs: 2.7g, Protein: 15g

36. Mint Avocado Chilled Soup

Servings: 2
Preparation time: 15 mins

Ingredients

- 2 romaine lettuce leaves
- 1 Tablespoon lime juice
- 1 medium ripe avocado
- 1 cup coconut milk, chilled
- 20 fresh mint leaves
- Salt to taste

Directions

1. Put all the ingredients in a blender and blend until smooth.
2. Refrigerate for about 10 minutes and serve chilled.

Nutrition Value: Calories: 432 Carbs: 16.1g Fats: 42.2g Proteins: 5.2g Sodium: 33mg Sugar: 4.5g

37. Easy Butternut Squash Soup

Servings: 4
Preparation time: 1 hour 45 mins

Ingredients

- 1 small onion, chopped
- 4 cups chicken broth
- 1 butternut squash
- 3 tablespoons coconut oil
- Salt, to taste
- Nutmeg and pepper, to taste

Directions

1. Put oil and onions in a large pot and add onions.
2. Sauté for about 3 minutes and add chicken broth and butternut squash.
3. Simmer for about 1 hour on medium heat and transfer into an immersion blender.
4. Pulse until smooth and season with salt, pepper and nutmeg.
5. Return to the pot and cook for about 30 minutes.
6. Dish out and serve hot.

Nutrition Value: Calories: 149 Carbs: 6.6g Fats: 11.6g Proteins: 5.4g Sodium: 765mg Sugar: 2.2g

38. Spring Soup Recipe with Poached Egg

Servings: 2
Preparation time: 20 mins

Ingredients

- 2 eggs
- 2 tablespoons butter
- 4 cups chicken broth
- 1 head of romaine lettuce, chopped
- Salt, to taste

Directions

1. Boil the chicken broth and lower heat.

2. Poach the eggs in the broth for about 5 minutes and remove the eggs.
3. Place each egg into a bowl and add chopped romaine lettuce into the broth.
4. Cook for about 10 minutes and ladle the broth with the lettuce into the bowls.

Nutrition Value: Calories: 264 Carbs: 7g Fats: 18.9g Proteins: 16.1g Sodium: 1679mg Sugar: 3.4g

39. Cauliflower, leek & bacon soup

Servings: 4
Preparation time: 10 mins

Ingredients
- 4 cups chicken broth
- ½ cauliflower head, chopped
- 1 leek, chopped
- Salt and black pepper, to taste
- 5 bacon strips

Directions
1. Put the cauliflower, leek and chicken broth into the pot and cook for about 1 hour on medium heat.
2. Transfer into an immersion blender and pulse until smooth.
3. Return the soup into the pot and microwave the bacon strips for 1 minute.
4. Cut the bacon into small pieces and put into the soup.
5. Cook on for about 30 minutes on low heat.
6. Season with salt and pepper and serve.

Nutrition Value: Calories: 185 Carbs: 5.8g Fats: 12.7g Proteins: 10.8g Sodium: 1153mg Sugar: 2.4g

40. Swiss Chard Egg Drop Soup

Servings: 4
Preparation time: 20 mins

Ingredients

- 3 cups bone broth
- 2 eggs, whisked
- 1 teaspoon ground oregano
- 3 tablespoons butter
- 2 cups Swiss chard, chopped
- 2 tablespoons coconut aminos
- 1 teaspoon ginger, grated
- Salt and black pepper, to taste

Directions

Heat the bone broth in a saucepan and add whisked eggs while stirring slowly.

1. Add the swiss chard, butter, coconut aminos, ginger, oregano and salt and black pepper.
2. Cook for about 10 minutes and serve hot.

Nutrition Value: Calories: 185 Carbs: 2.9g Fats: 11g Proteins: 18.3g Sodium: 252mg Sugar: 0.4g

41. Mushroom Spinach Soup

Servings: 4
Preparation time: 25 mins

Ingredients

- 1cupspinach,cleaned and chopped
- 100gmushrooms,chopped
- 1onion
- 6 garlic cloves
- ½ teaspoon red chili powder
- Salt and black pepper, to taste

- 3 tablespoons buttermilk
- 1 teaspoon almond flour
- 2 cups chicken broth
- 3 tablespoons butter
- ¼ cup fresh cream,for garnish

Directions

1. Heat butter in a pan and add onions and garlic.
2. Sauté for about 3 minutes and add spinach, salt and red chili powder.
3. Sauté for about 4 minutes and add mushrooms.
4. Transfer into a blender and blend to make a puree.
5. Return to the pan and add buttermilk and almond flour for creamy texture.
6. Mix well and simmer for about 2 minutes.
7. Garnish with fresh cream and serve hot.

Nutrition Value: Calories: 160 Carbs: 7g Fats: 13.3g Proteins: 4.7g Sodium: 462mg Sugar: 2.7g

42. Delicata Squash Soup

Servings: 5
Preparation time: 45mins

Ingredients

- 1½ cups beef bone broth
- 1small onion, peeled and grated.
- ½ teaspoon sea salt
- ¼ teaspoon poultry seasoning
- 2small Delicata Squash, chopped
- 2 garlic cloves, minced
- 2tablespoons olive oil
- ¼ teaspoon black pepper
- 1 small lemon, juiced

- 5 tablespoons sour cream

Directions
1. Put Delicata Squash and water in a medium pan and bring to a boil.
2. Reduce the heat and cook for about 20 minutes.
3. Drain and set aside.
4. Put olive oil, onions, garlic and poultry seasoning in a small sauce pan.
5. Cook for about 2 minutes and add broth.
6. Allow it to simmer for 5 minutes and remove from heat.
7. Whisk in the lemon juice and transfer the mixture in a blender.
8. Pulse until smooth and top with sour cream.

Nutrition Value: Calories: 109 Carbs: 4.9g Fats: 8.5g Proteins: 3g Sodium: 279mg Sugar: 2.4g

43. Broccoli Soup

Servings: 6
Preparation time: 10 mins

Ingredients
- 3 tablespoons ghee
- 5 garlic cloves
- 1 teaspoon sage
- ¼ teaspoon ginger
- 2 cups broccoli
- 1 small onion
- 1 teaspoon oregano
- ½ teaspoon parsley
- Salt and black pepper, to taste
- 6 cups vegetable broth

- 4 tablespoons butter

Directions

1. Put ghee, onions, spices and garlic in a pot and cook for 3 minutes.
2. Add broccoli and cook for about 4 minutes.
3. Add vegetable broth, cover and allow it to simmer for about 30 minutes.
4. Transfer into a blender and blend until smooth.
5. Add the butter to give it a creamy delicious texture and flavor

Nutrition Value: Calories: 183 Carbs: 5.2g Fats: 15.6g Proteins: 6.1g Sodium: 829mg Sugar: 1.8g

44. Apple Pumpkin Soup

Servings: 8
Preparation time: 10 mins

Ingredients

- 1 apple, chopped
- 1 whole kabocha pumpkin, peeled, seeded and cubed
- 1 cup almond flour
- ¼ cup ghee
- 1 pinch cardamom powder
- 2 quarts water
- ¼ cup coconut cream
- 1 pinch ground black pepper

Directions

1. Heat ghee in the bottom of a heavy pot and add apples.
2. Cook for about 5 minutes on a medium flame and add pumpkin.
3. Sauté for about 3 minutes and add almond flour.
4. Sauté for about 1 minute and add water.

5. Lower the flame and cook for about 30 minutes.
6. Transfer the soup into an immersion blender and blend until smooth.
7. Top with coconut cream and serve.

Nutrition Value: Calories: 186 Carbs: 10.4g Fats: 14.9g Proteins: 3.7g Sodium: 7mg Sugar: 5.4g

45. Keto French Onion Soup

Servings: 6
Preparation time: 40 mins

Ingredients
- 5 tablespoons butter
- 500 g brown onion medium
- 4 drops liquid stevia
- 4 tablespoons olive oil
- 3 cups beef stock

Directions
1. Put the butter and olive oil in a large pot over medium low heat and add onions and salt.
2. Cook for about 5 minutes and stir in stevia.
3. Cook for another 5 minutes and add beef stock.
4. Reduce the heat to low and simmer for about 25 minutes.
5. Dish out into soup bowls and serve hot.

Nutrition Value: Calories: 198 Carbs: 6g Fats: 20.6g Proteins: 2.9g Sodium: 883mg Sugar: 1.7g

46. Cauliflower and Thyme Soup

Servings: 6
Preparation time: 30 mins

Ingredients

- 2teaspoonsthyme powder
- 1head cauliflower
- 3cupsvegetable stock
- ½ teaspoon matcha green tea powder
- 3tablespoonsolive oil
- Salt and black pepper, to taste
- 5garlic cloves,chopped

Directions

1. Put the vegetable stock, thyme and matcha powder to a large pot over medium-high heat and bring to a boil.
2. Add cauliflower and cook for about 10 minutes.
3. Meanwhile, put the olive oil and garlic in a small sauce pan and cook for about 1 minute.
4. Add the garlic, salt and black pepper and cook for about 2 minutes.
5. Transfer into an immersion blender and blend until smooth.
6. Dish out and serve immediately.

Nutrition Value: Calories: 79 Carbs: 3.8g Fats: 7.1g Proteins: 1.3g Sodium: 39mg Sugar: 1.5g

47. Homemade Thai Chicken Soup

Servings: 12
Preparation time: 8 hours 25 mins

Ingredients

- 1 lemongrass stalk, cut into large chunks
- 5 thick slices of fresh ginger
- 1 whole chicken
- 20 fresh basil leaves
- 1 lime, juiced

- 1 tablespoon salt

Directions

1. Place the chicken, 10 basil leaves, lemongrass, ginger, salt and water into the slow cooker.
2. Cook for about 8 hours on low and dish out into a bowl.
3. Stir in fresh lime juice and basil leaves to serve.

Nutrition Value: Calories: 255 Carbs: 1.2g Fats: 17.6g Proteins: 25.2g Sodium: 582mg Sugar: 0.1g

48. Chicken Kale Soup

Servings: 6
Preparation time: 6 hours 10 mins

Ingredients

- 2poundschicken breast, skinless
- 3cuponion
- 1tablespoonolive oil
- 14ounceschicken bone broth
- ½ cup olive oil
- 4 cups chicken stock
- ¼ cup lemon juice
- 5ouncesbaby kale leaves
- Salt, to taste

Directions

1. Season chicken with salt and black pepper.
2. Heat olive oil over medium heat in a large skillet and add seasoned chicken.
3. Reduce the temperature and cook for about 15 minutes.
4. Shred the chicken and place in the crock pot.
5. Process the chicken broth and onions in a blender and

blend until smooth.

6. Pour into crock pot and stir in the remaining ingredients.
7. Cook on low for about 6 hours, stirring once while cooking.

Nutrition Value: Calories: 261 Carbs: 2g Fats: 21g Proteins: 14.1g Sodium: 264mg Sugar: 0.3g

49. Chicken Veggie Soup

Servings: 6
Preparation time: 20 mins

Ingredients

- 5 chicken thighs
- 12 cups water
- 1 tablespoon adobo seasoning
- 4 celery ribs
- 1 yellow onion
- 1½ teaspoons whole black peppercorns
- 6 sprigs fresh parsley
- 2 teaspoons coarse sea salt
- 2 carrots
- 6 mushrooms, sliced
- 2 garlic cloves
- 1 bay leaf
- 3 sprigs fresh thyme

1. **Directions**
2. Put water, chicken thighs, carrots, celery ribs, onion, garlic cloves and herbs in a large pot.
3. Bring to a boil and reduce the heat to low.
4. Cover the pot and simmer for about 30 minutes.
5. Dish out the chicken and shred it, removing the bones.

6. Put the bones back into the pot and simmer for about 20 minutes.
7. Strain the broth, discarding the chunks and put the liquid back into the pot.
8. Bring it to a boil and simmer for about 30 minutes.
9. Put the mushrooms in the broth and simmer for about 10 minutes.
10. Dish out to serve hot.

Nutrition Value: Calories: 250 Carbs: 6.4g Fats: 8.9g Proteins: 35.1g Sodium: 852mg Sugar: 2.5g

50. Chicken Mulligatawny Soup

Servings: 10
Preparation time: 30 mins

Ingredients

- 1½ tablespoons curry powder
- 3 cups celery root, diced
- 2 tablespoons Swerve
- 10 cups chicken broth
- 5 cups chicken, chopped and cooked
- ¼ cup apple cider
- ½ cup sour cream
- ¼ cup fresh parsley, chopped
- 2 tablespoons butter
- Salt and black pepper, to taste

Directions

1. Combine the broth, butter, chicken, curry powder, celery root and apple cider in a large soup pot.
2. Bring to a boil and simmer for about 30 minutes.
3. Stir in Swerve, sour cream, fresh parsley, salt and black pepper.
4. Dish out and serve hot.

Nutrition Value: Calories: 215 Carbs: 7.1g Fats: 8.5g Proteins: 26.4g Sodium: 878mg Sugar: 2.2g

51. Buffalo Ranch Chicken Soup

Servings: 4
Preparation time: 40 mins

Ingredients

- 2 tablespoons parsley
- 2 celery stalks, chopped
- 6 tablespoons butter
- 1 cup heavy whipping cream
- 4 cups chicken, cooked and shredded
- 4 tablespoons ranch dressing
- ¼ cup yellow onions, chopped
- 8 oz cream cheese
- 8 cups chicken broth
- 7 hearty bacon slices, crumbled

Directions

1. Heat butter in a pan and add chicken.
2. Cook for about 5 minutes and add 1½ cups water.
3. Cover and cook for about 10 minutes.
4. Put the chicken and rest of the ingredients into the saucepan except parsley and cook for about 10 minutes.
5. Top with parsley and serve hot.

Nutrition Value: Calories: 444 Carbs: 4g Fats: 34g Proteins: 28g Sodium: 1572mg Sugar: 2g

52. Traditional Chicken Soup

Servings: 6
Preparation time: 1 hour 45 mins

Ingredients

- 3 pounds chicken
- 4 quarts water
- 4 stalks celery
- 3 large red onion
- 1 large carrot
- 3 garlic cloves
- 2 thyme sprigs
- 2 rosemary sprigs
- Salt and black pepper, to taste

Directions

1. Put water and chicken in the stock pot on medium high heat.
2. Bring to a boil and allow it to simmer for about 10 minutes.
3. Add onion, garlic, celery, salt and pepper and simmer on medium low heat for 30 minutes.
4. Add thyme and carrots and simmer on low for another 30 minutes.
5. Dish out the chicken and shred the pieces, removing the bones.
6. Return the chicken pieces to the pot and add rosemary sprigs.
7. Simmer for about 20 minutes at low heat and dish out to serve.

Nutrition Value: Calories: 357 Carbs: 3.3g Fats: 7g Proteins: 66.2g Sodium: 175mg Sugar: 1.1g

53. Chicken Noodle Soup

Servings: 6
Preparation time: 30 mins

Ingredients

- 1 onion, minced
- 1 rib celery, sliced
- 3 cups chicken, shredded
- 3 eggs, lightly beaten
- 1 green onion, for garnish
- 2 tablespoons coconut oil
- 1 carrot, peeled and thinly sliced
- 2 teaspoons dried thyme
- 2½ quarts homemade bone broth
- ¼ cup fresh parsley, minced
- Salt and black pepper, to taste

Directions

1. Heat coconut oil over medium-high heat in a large pot and add onions, carrots, and celery.
2. Cook for about 4 minutes and stir in the bone broth, thyme and chicken.
3. Simmer for about 15 minutes and stir in parsley.
4. Pour beaten eggs into the soup in a slow steady stream.
5. Remove soup from heat and let it stand for about 2 minutes.
6. Season with salt and black pepper and dish out to serve.

Nutrition Value: Calories: 226 Carbs: 3.5g Fats: 8.9g Proteins: 31.8g Sodium: 152mg Sugar: 1.6g

54. Chicken Cabbage Soup

Servings: 8
Preparation time: 35 mins

Ingredients

- 2celery stalks

- 2garlic cloves, minced
- 4 oz.butter
- 6 oz. mushrooms, sliced
- 2 tablespoons onions, dried and minced
- 1 teaspoon salt
- 8 cups chicken broth
- 1medium carrot
- 2 cups green cabbage, sliced into strips
- 2 teaspoons dried parsley
- ¼ teaspoon black pepper
- 1½ rotisserie chickens, shredded

Directions

1. Melt butter in a large pot and add celery, mushrooms, onions and garlic into the pot.
2. Cook for about 4 minutes and add broth, parsley, carrot, salt and black pepper.
3. Simmer for about 10 minutes and add cooked chicken and cabbage.
4. Simmer for an additional 12 minutes until the cabbage is tender.
5. Dish out and serve hot.

Nutrition Value: Calories: 184 Carbs: 4.2g Fats: 13.1g Proteins: 12.6g Sodium: 1244mg Sugar: 2.1g

55. Green Chicken Enchilada Soup

Servings: 5
Preparation time: 20 mins

Ingredients

- 4 oz. cream cheese, softened
- ½ cup salsa verde
- 1 cup cheddar cheese, shredded

- 2 cups cooked chicken, shredded
- 2 cups chicken stock

Directions

1. Put salsa verde, cheddar cheese, cream cheese and chicken stock in an immersion blender and blend until smooth.
2. Pour this mixture into a medium saucepan and cook for about 5 minutes on medium heat.
3. Add the shredded chicken and cook for about 5 minutes.
4. Garnish with additional shredded cheddar and serve hot.

Nutrition Value: Calories: 265 Carbs: 2.2g Fats: 17.4g Proteins: 24.2g Sodium: 686mg Sugar: 0.8g

56. Keto BBQ Chicken Pizza Soup

Servings: 6
Preparation time: 1 hour 30 mins

Ingredients

- 6 chicken legs
- 1 medium red onion, diced
- 4 garlic cloves
- 1 large tomato, unsweetened
- 4 cups green beans
- ¾ cup BBQ Sauce
- 1½ cups mozzarella cheese, shredded
- ¼ cup ghee
- 2 quarts water
- 2 quarts chicken stock
- Salt and black pepper, to taste
- Fresh cilantro, for garnishing

Directions

1. Put chicken, water and salt in a large pot and bring to a boil.
2. Reduce the heat to medium-low and cook for about 75 minutes.
3. Shred the meat off the bones using a fork and keep aside.
4. Put ghee, red onions and garlic in a large soup and cook over a medium heat.
5. Add chicken stock and bring to a boil over a high heat.
6. Add green beans and tomato to the pot and cook for about 15 minutes.
7. AddBBQ Sauce, shredded chicken, salt and black pepper to the pot.
8. Ladle the soup into serving bowls and top with shredded mozzarella cheese and cilantro to serve.

Nutrition Value: Calories: 449 Carbs: 7.1g Fats: 32.5g Proteins: 30.8g Sodium: 252mg Sugar: 4.7g

57. Salmon Stew Soup

Servings: 5
Preparation time: 25 mins

Ingredients

- 4 cups chicken broth
- 3 salmon fillets, chunked
- 2 tablespoons butter
- 1 cup parsley, chopped
- 3 cups Swiss chard, roughly chopped
- 2 Italian squash, chopped
- 1 garlic clove, crushed
- ½ lemon, juiced
- Salt and black pepper, to taste

- 2 eggs

Directions

1. Put the chicken broth and garlic into a pot and bring to a boil.
2. Add salmon, lemon juice and butter in the pot and cook for about 10 minutes on medium heat.
3. Add Swiss chard, Italian squash, salt and pepper and cook for about 10 minutes.
4. Whisk eggs and add to the pot, stirring continuously.
5. Garnish with parsley and serve.

Nutrition Value: Calories: 262 Carbs: 7.8g Fats: 14g Proteins: 27.5g Sodium: 1021mg Sugar: 1.2g

58. Spicy Halibut Tomato Soup

Servings: 8
Preparation time: 1 hour 5mins

Ingredients

- 2garliccloves, minced
- 1tablespoonolive oil
- ¼ cup fresh parsley, chopped
- 10anchoviescanned in oil, minced
- 6cupsvegetable broth
- 1teaspoonblack pepper
- 1poundhalibut fillets, chopped
- 3tomatoes, peeled and diced
- 1teaspoonsalt
- 1teaspoonred chili flakes

Directions

1. Heat olive oil in a large stockpot over medium heat and add garlic and half of the parsley.
2. Add anchovies, tomatoes, vegetable broth, red chili

flakes, salt and black pepper and bring to a boil.

3. Reduce the heat to medium-low and simmer for about 20 minutes.
4. Add halibut fillets and cook for about 10 minutes.
5. Dish out the halibut and shred into small pieces.
6. Mix back with the soup and garnish with the remaining fresh parsley to serve.

Nutrition Value: Calories: 170 Carbs: 3g Fats: 6.7g Proteins: 23.4g Sodium: 2103mg Sugar: 1.8g

59. Spicy Shrimp and Chorizo Soup

Servings: 8
Preparation time: 55mins

Ingredients
- 2 tablespoons butter
- 1medium onion, diced
- 3celery ribs, diced
- 4 garlic cloves, sliced
- 12ounces chorizo, diced
- 2tomatoes, diced
- 1½teaspoons smoked paprika
- 1teaspoonground coriander
- 1teaspoonsea salt
- 1quart chicken broth
- 1poundshrimp,peeled, deveined and chopped
- 2tablespoons fresh cilantro, minced
- 1avocado,diced
- Chopped fresh cilantro,for garnish

Directions
1. Heat half of butter over medium-high heat in a large pot and add celery, bell pepper and onions.

2. Cook for about 8 minutes, stirring occasionally and add tomato paste, half of chorizo, garlic, coriander, smoked paprika and salt.
3. Cook for about 1 minute, stirring continuously and add the tomatoes and broth.
4. Cook for about 20 minutes and heat remaining butter in a small pan.
5. Add remaining chorizo and cook for about 5 minutes until crispy.
6. Add smoked paprika, shrimp, coriander and simmer for about 4 minutes.
7. Remove from the heat and stir in minced cilantro.
8. Top with the crispy chorizo and chopped cilantro and serve.

Nutrition Value: Calories: 374 Carbs: 7.9g Fats: 25.9g Proteins: 26.8g Sodium: 1315mg Sugar: 2.1g

60. Creamy Leek & Salmon Soup

Servings: 4
Preparation time: 30 mins

Ingredients
- 2 tablespoons butter
- 2 leeks, washed, trimmed and sliced
- 3 garlic cloves, minced
- 6 cups seafood broth
- 2 teaspoons dried thyme leaves
- 1 pound salmon, in bite size pieces
- 1½ cups coconut milk
- Salt and black pepper, to taste

Directions
1. Heat butter at a low-medium heat in a large saucepan and add garlic and leeks.

2. Cook for about 3 minutes and add stock and thyme.
3. Simmer for about 15 minutes and season with salt and black pepper.
4. Add salmon and coconut milk to the pan and simmer for about 5 minutes.
5. Dish out and serve immediately.

Nutrition Value: Calories: 332 Carbs: 9.1g Fats: 24.3g Proteins: 21.5g Sodium: 839mg Sugar: 3.9g

61. Thai Coconut Shrimp Soup

Servings: 5
Preparation time: 40 mins

Ingredients

BROTH
- 4 cups chicken broth
- 1½ cups full fat coconut milk
- 1 organic lime zest
- 1 teaspoondried lemongrass
- 1 cup fresh cilantro
- 1 jalapeno pepper, sliced
- 1 inch piece fresh ginger root
- 1 teaspoon sea salt

SOUP
- 100 grams raw shrimp
- 1 tablespoon coconut oil
- 30 grams mushrooms, sliced
- 1 red onion, thinly sliced
- 1 anchovy, finely smashed
- 1 lime, juiced
- 1 tablespoon cilantro, chopped

Directions

1. Broth: Mix together all the ingredients in a sauce pan and simmer for about 20 minutes.
2. Strain the mixture through a fine mesh colander and pour back into the pan.
3. Soup: Simmer the broth again and add shrimp, onions, mushrooms and anchovy.
4. Allow it to simmer for about 10 minutes and add lime juice.
5. Garnish with cilantro and serve hot.

Nutrition Value: Calories: 247 Carbs: 7.7g Fats: 19g Proteins: 11.5g Sodium: 1061mg Sugar: 3.2g

62. Salmon Head Soup

Servings: 6
Preparation time: 2 hours 45 mins

Ingredients

- 2 salmon heads
- 1 small onion, sliced
- 1 bulb green garlic, minced
- ½ cup wakame
- 2 tablespoons ginger, peeled and minced
- ¼ cup mirin
- ¼ cup coconut aminos
- 2 zucchinis, spiraled into noodles
- Chives and chilies, for garnish

Directions

1. Put salmon heads, ginger and water in a slow cooker and cook on high for about 2 hours.
2. Strain broth and shredded shrimp meat and transfer into a stock pot along with green garlic, ginger, onions, mirin, wakame and coconut aminos.

3. Cook for about 20 minutes and add zucchinis.
4. Cook for about 15 minutes and garnish with chives and chillies.

Nutrition Value: Calories: 123 Carbs: 7g Fats: 5.8g Proteins: 9.6g Sodium: 163mg Sugar: 3.3g

63. Carrot Ginger Halibut Soup

Servings: 6
Preparation time: 45 mins

Ingredients
- 1 large onion, chopped
- 2 tablespoons fresh ginger, peeled and minced
- 1 tablespoon coconut oil
- 4 carrots, peeled and sliced
- 2 cups chicken broth
- 1 cup water
- ½ teaspoon black pepper
- 1 pound halibut, cut into 1" chunks
- Sea salt, to taste

Directions
1. Heat coconut oil over medium heat in a large pot and add onions.
2. Sauté for about 8 minutes and add ginger, carrots, broth and water.
3. Bring to a boil, reduce heat and simmer for about 20 minutes.
4. Transfer into an immersion blender and blend until smooth.
5. Return the soup to the pot and add halibut, sea salt and black pepper.
6. Allow to simmer for 5 more minutes and serve.

Nutrition Value: Calories: 246 Carbs: 8g Fats: 16.3g Proteins: 16.3g Sodium: 363mg Sugar: 3.4g

64. Coconut Seafood Soup

Servings: 5
Preparation time: 30 mins

Ingredients

- 10 button mushrooms, sliced
- 1 cup romaine lettuce, chopped
- 4 cups chicken stock
- ½ cup kale, chopped
- 4 tilapia filets, chopped into large chunks
- 10 prawns
- 1 cup coconut cream
- Salt, to taste
- 10 mussels
- 1 teaspoon Red Boat fish sauce

Directions

1. Put the chicken stock into a large pot and bring to the boil.
2. Add kale, romaine lettuce and mushrooms and boil again.
3. Add tilapia pieces and prawns and bring to the boil again.
4. Boil for around 5 minutes and add coconut cream, fish sauce and salt.
5. Stir gently and dish out to serve immediately.

Nutrition Value: Calories: 300 Carbs: 7.3g Fats: 15.5g Proteins: 34.7g Sodium: 1217mg Sugar: 2.9g

65. Cheesy Shrimp Soup

Servings: 8

Preparation time: 30 mins

Ingredients

- 8 oz cheddar cheese, shredded
- 24 oz extra small shrimp
- 2 cups mushrooms, sliced
- 32 oz chicken broth
- ½ cup butter
- 1 cup heavy whipping cream

Directions

1. Put chicken broth and mushrooms to a large soup pot and bring to a boil.
2. Reduce heat and stir in butter, heavy whipping cream and cheese.
3. Add shrimp and allow it to simmer for about 15 minutes.
4. Dish out and serve hot.

Nutrition Value: Calories: 395 Carbs: 3.3g Fats: 28.7g Proteins: 29.8g Sodium: 1428mg Sugar: 0.8g

66. Thai Hot and Sour Shrimp Soup

Servings: 6
Preparation time: 55 mins

Ingredients

- 3 tablespoons butter
- 1 inch piece ginger root, peeled
- 2teaspoon fresh lime zest
- 5 cups chicken broth
- 1 small green zucchini
- 1 pound shrimps, peeled and deveined
- 1 medium onion, diced

- 4 garlic cloves
- 1 lemongrass stalk
- 1 red Thai chili, roughly chopped
- 2pound cremini mushrooms, sliced into wedges
- 2 tablespoons fresh lime juice
- 2 tablespoons fish sauce
- 4bunch fresh Thai basil, coarsely chopped
- 4bunch fresh cilantro, coarsely chopped
- Salt and black pepper, to taste

Directions
1. Heat butter in a large pot over medium heat and add shrimps.
2. Stir well and add garlic, onions, ginger, lemongrass, lime zest, Thai chillies, salt and black pepper.
3. Cook for about 3 minutes and add chicken broth to the pot.
4. Simmer for about 30 minutes and strain it.
5. Heat a large sauté pan over high heat and add coconut oil, mushrooms, zucchini, salt and black pepper.
6. Sauté for about 3 minutes and add to the shrimp mixture.
7. Simmer for about 2 minutes and add fish sauce, lime juice, salt and black pepper.
8. Cook for about 1 minute and add fresh cilantro and basil.
9. Dish out and serve hot.

Nutrition Value: Calories: 223 Carbs: 8.7g Fats: 10.2g Proteins: 23g Sodium: 1128mg Sugar: 3.6g

67. Creamy Pulled Pork Soup

Servings: 6
Preparation time: 55 mins

Ingredients

- 1 medium onion
- 1 pound cauliflower
- ½ cup butter
- 8 garlic cloves
- 1 teaspoon sea salt
- 7 cups chicken broth
- 1½ cups pulled pork
- 2 teaspoons dried oregano
- 3 tablespoons sour cream

Directions

1. Heat butter in a saucepan and add onions and garlic.
2. Sauté for about 3 minutes and add cauliflower, chicken broth and sea salt.
3. Cook for about 20 minutes and transfer it to an immersion blender.
4. Blend until smooth and add dried oregano.
5. Return to the saucepan and simmer for about 5 minutes.
6. Add sour cream and pulled pork and cook for about 15 minutes.
7. Dish out and serve hot.

Nutrition Value: Calories: 257 Carbs: 8.7g Fats: 19.1g Proteins: 13.6g Sodium: 1351mg Sugar: 3.5g

68. Thai Beef and Broccoli Soup

Servings: 8
Preparation time: 50 mins

Ingredients

- 1 onion, chopped
- 2 garlic cloves, minced

- 2 tablespoons avocado oil
- 2 tablespoons Thai green curry paste
- 2-inch ginger, minced
- 1 Serrano pepper, minced
- 3 tablespoons coconut aminos
- ½ teaspoon salt
- 4 cups beef bone broth
- 1 cup full-fatcoconut milk
- 1 pound ground beef
- 2 teaspoons fish sauce
- ½ teaspoon black pepper
- 2 large broccoli stalks, cut into florets
- Cilantro, garnish

Directions
1. Put avocado oil and onions into a large pot and sauté for about 4 minutes.
2. Add ginger, garlic, Serrano pepper and curry paste and cook for about 1 minute.
3. Add coconut aminos, fish sauce, ground beef, salt and black pepper.
4. Cook for about 6 minutes and add bone broth.
5. Reduce the heat to low and cook, covered for about 20 minutes.
6. Add coconut milk and broccoli florets to the pot and cover.
7. Cook for another 10 minutes and increase heat to high.
8. Simmer for about 5 minutes and garnish with cilantro to serve.

Nutrition Value: Calories: 240 Carbs: 8.5g Fats: 13.5g Proteins: 22g Sodium: 547mg Sugar: 2.2g

69. Good Ole' Southern Potlikker Soup

Servings: 6
Preparation time: 10 mins

Ingredients

- 1 large onion, diced
- 2 garlic cloves, minced
- 6 cups chicken broth
- 4 tablespoons butter
- 1 pound ham steaks, cubed
- 2 celery stalks, chopped
- 1 cup kale, chopped
- 1 tablespoon apple cider vinegar
- 6 cups collards, chopped
- 1 tablespoon Sriracha
- Salt and black pepper, to taste

Directions

1. Put butter, ham, garlic, onions, carrots and celery in a heavy-bottomed pot.
2. Cook for about 3 minutes over medium heat and add rest of the ingredients.
3. Bring to a boil and reduce the heat.
4. Simmer for about 90 minutes and dish out to serve.

Nutrition Value: Calories: 160 Carbs: 7.6g Fats: 10.3g Proteins: 9.4g Sodium: 1055mg Sugar: 2g

70. Potsticker Meatball Asian Noodle Soup

Servings: 6
Preparation time: 35 mins

Ingredients

For the meatballs:

- 1 egg

- 1 pound ground pork
- 3 cup almond flour
- ½ teaspoon garlic powder
- 1 teaspoon ginger, minced
- 1 tablespoon gluten free soy sauce
- ½ teaspoon kosher salt

For the broth:
- 2 tablespoons ginger, minced
- 1 teaspoon sesame oil
- 1 teaspoon garlic, minced
- 2 cups water
- 1 tablespoon fish sauce
- ½ teaspoon kosher salt
- 4 cups chicken broth
- 1 tablespoon gluten free soy sauce
- ½ teaspoon red pepper flakes
- To assemble the soup:
- 2 cups Napa cabbage, shredded
- 3 cups shiratake noodles, drained and rinsed
- ¼ cup radish sticks
- 6 lime wedges
- ½ cup cilantro, chopped

Directions
1. For the meatballs: Mix together all the ingredients for meatballs in a medium bowl.
2. Make meatballs out of this mixture and transfer on to a baking sheet.
3. Bake for about 12 minutes at 375 degrees F and dish out.
4. For the broth: Heat sesame oil and add ginger and garlic

5. Cook for about 1 minute and add water, soy sauce, chicken broth, red pepper flakes, fish sauce and salt.
6. Bring to a boil and simmer for about 10 minutes.
7. Strain the broth and return to the pan.
8. Bring to a boil right before serving.
9. To assemble the soup: Place about ½ cup shiratake noodles in a soup bowl and top with a handful of cabbage, four meatballs, a pinch of radish and cilantro.
10. Ladle about 1 cup of hot broth into each bowl and squeeze a lime wedge over it.

Nutrition Value: Calories: 226 Carbs: 7.9g Fats: 8.7g Proteins: 27.4g Sodium: 1476mg Sugar: 1.3g

71. Beef Noodle Soup with Shitake Mushrooms and Baby Bok Choy

Servings: 1
Preparation time: 25 mins

Ingredients

- 2 teaspoons garlic, minced
- ¼ teaspoon crushed red pepper flakes
- ½ large zucchini, peeled and spiralized
- 3 oz beef steaks, cut into 1" cubes
- 2 tablespoons olive oil
- 1 cup chicken broth, homemade
- 1 head of baby bokchoy, roughly chopped
- ¼ cup green onions, chopped
- ¼ cup water
- 1 tablespoon coconut aminos
- ½ cup mushrooms
- Salt and black pepper, to taste

Directions

1. Season the beef cubes with 1 teaspoon olive oil, salt and black pepper.
2. Heat 1 tablespoon of olive oil over medium heat in a large saucepan and add garlic.
3. Sauté for about 1 minute and add beef.
4. Cook for about 2 minutes on each side and dish out.
5. Add remaining oil in the same saucepan and add mushrooms, bokchoy and red pepper flakes.
6. Stir to combine and cook for about 2 minutes.
7. Add chicken broth and water and bring to a boil.
8. Add coconut aminos and reduce heat to low.
9. Simmer for about 5 minutes and add zucchini noodles, beef and half of the green onions.
10. Cook for about 2 minutes and dish out into a bowl.
11. Top with remaining green onions and serve.

Nutrition Value: Calories: 252 Carbs: 7.2g Fats: 17.6g Proteins: 17.7g Sodium: 262mg Sugar: 2.6g

72. Thai Tom Saap Pork Ribs Soup

Servings: 6
Preparation time: 2 hours

Ingredients
- 1 red shallot, chopped
- 1 pound pork spare ribs
- 4 small lemongrass stalks, chopped
- 8 cups water
- 1 lime, juiced
- 2 tablespoons fish sauce
- 3 tablespoons ginger
- 10 kaffir lime leaves
- Salt,to taste

Directions

1. Put the pork spare ribs into a large pot of water and bring to a boil.
2. Cook for about 10 minutes and pour out the liquid with the froth.
3. Pour water, lemongrass, shallots, ginger and salt to the pot and simmer for about 1 hour on low heat.
4. Add kaffir lime leaves, fish sauce, lime juice and salt and dish out to serve.

Nutrition Value: Calories: 232 Carbs: 8.9g Fats: 16.4g Proteins: 12.2g Sodium: 424mg Sugar: 0.3g

73. Creamy Cauliflower & Ham Soup

Servings: 10
Preparation time: 10 mins

Ingredients
- 6 cups chicken broth
- ½ teaspoon onion powder
- 2 tablespoons apple cider vinegar
- 24 oz cauliflower florets
- 2 cups water
- ½ teaspoon garlic powder
- 3 cups ham, chopped
- 1 tablespoon fresh thyme leaves
- 3 tablespoons butter
- Salt and black pepper, to taste

Directions
1. Mix together garlic powder, chicken broth, cauliflower, water and onion powder in a large soup pot.
2. Bring to a boil and simmer for about 30 minutes.
3. Transfer into an immersion blender and blend until smooth.
4. Return to the pot and stir in ham and thyme leaves.

5. Simmer for about 10 minutes and add butter and apple cider vinegar.
6. Remove from the heat and season with salt and black pepper.
7. Dish out and serve hot.

Nutrition Value: Calories: 139 Carbs: 6.1g Fats: 7.9g Proteins: 11.1g Sodium: 1033mg Sugar: 2.1g

74. Bacon and Pumpkin Soup

Servings: 6
Preparation time: 4 hours 15 mins

Ingredients

- 400gpumpkin,diced
- 3 cups bacon hock, diced
- Boiling water

Directions

1. Place pumpkin, boiling water and bacon hock in the slow cooker.
2. Cook on HIGH for about 4 hours and pull the meat away from the bones.
3. Return the meat to the slow cooker and allow it to simmer for 5 minutes before serving.

Nutrition Value: Calories: 116 Carbs: 3.2g Fats: 5.9g Proteins: 12.1g Sodium: 27mg Sugar: 1.3g

75. Quick Italian Sausage and Pepper Soup

Servings: 10
Preparation time: 6 hours 20 mins

Ingredients

- 2pounds hot Italian sausage,cut into bite size pieces
- 2sweet bell peppers, chopped

- 2cupschicken broth low sodium
- 2tablespoonsextra virgin olive oil
- 4 garliccloves, minced
- 1onion, chopped
- 2tablespoonsred wine vinegar
- 2cupswater
- 1teaspoondried parsley
- 4ouncesfresh spinach leaves
- 1(28 ounce) can diced tomatoes with juice
- 1teaspoondried basil
- ½ cup Parmesan cheese, grated

Directions

1. Heat olive oil in a large skillet and add sausages.
2. Cook for about 5 minutes until browned and transfer into a slow cooker.
3. Add the remaining ingredients except spinach and fresh herbs.
4. Cook on LOW for about 6 hours.
5. Add fresh herbs and spinach and serve.

Nutrition Value: Calories: 373 Carbs: 6.9g Fats: 29.4g Proteins: 20.4g Sodium: 845mg Sugar: 3.8g

76. Pork and Tomato Soup

Servings: 8
Preparation time: 45 mins

Ingredients

- 2 tablespoons olive oil
- ½ cup onions, chopped
- 2 pounds boneless pork ribs, cut into 1 inch pieces
- 1 tablespoon garlic, chopped
- ½ cup dry white wine

- 1 cup chicken stock
- 1 cup water
- 2 cups cauliflower, finely chopped
- 2 cups fresh tomatoes, chopped
- 2 tablespoons fresh oregano, chopped
- Salt and black pepper, to taste

Directions

1. Season the pork generously with salt and black pepper.
2. Heat olive oil in a heavy saucepan and add seasoned pork.
3. Cook for about 3 minutes per side until browned and add garlic and onions.
4. Cook for about 2 minutes and add the chicken stock, white wine, fresh tomatoes and water.
5. Bring to a boil and pour into a slow cooker.
6. Cook on HIGH for about 4 hours until the meat is tender.
7. Stir in the cauliflower and fresh oregano and cook for another 20 minutes.
8. Dish out and serve hot.

Nutrition Value: Calories: 228 Carbs: 5.3g Fats: 7.8g Proteins: 31g Sodium: 172mg Sugar: 2.4g

77. Mint Avocado Chilled Soup

Servings: 2
Preparation time: 10 mins

Ingredients

- 2 romaine lettuce leaves
- 1 medium ripe avocado
- 1 cup coconut milk, chilled
- 20 fresh mint leaves

- 1 tablespoon lime juice
- Salt, to taste

Directions
1. Put all the ingredients into a blender and blend until smooth.
2. Refrigerate for about 10 minutes and serve chilled.

Nutrition Value: Calories: 245 Carbs: 8.4g Fats: 24.2g Proteins: 2.6g Sodium: 15mg Sugar: 2.3g

78. Chilled Zucchini Soup

Servings: 5
Preparation time: 10 mins

Ingredients
- 1 medium zucchini, cut into ½ inch pieces
- 4cupschicken broth
- 8ozcream cheese,cut into cubes
- ½ teaspoon ground cumin
- Salt and black pepper, to taste

Directions
1. Mix chicken broth and zucchini in a large stockpot.
2. Bring to a boil and reduce heat to low.
3. Simmer for about 10 minutes and add cream cheese.
4. Stir well and transfer to an immersion blender.
5. Blend until smooth and season with cumin, salt and black pepper.
6. Refrigerate to chill for about 2 hours and serve.

Nutrition Value: Calories: 196 Carbs: 3.4g Fats: 17g Proteins: 7.8g Sodium: 749mg Sugar: 1.3g

79. Super Food Keto Soup

Servings: 7
Preparation time: 30 mins

Ingredients

- 1 medium white onion, diced
- 1 bay leaf, crumbled
- 200 g fresh spinach
- 1 medium head cauliflower
- 2 garlic cloves
- 150 g watercress
- 4 cups vegetable stock
- 4cupghee
- 1 cup coconut cream
- Salt and black pepper, to taste

Directions

1. Put ghee, onions and garlic in a soup pot over medium-high heat.
2. Cook until golden brown and add cauliflower and bay leaf.
3. Cook for about 5 minutes and add the spinach and watercress.
4. Cook for about 3 minutes and pour in the vegetable stock.
5. Bring to a boil and add coconut cream.
6. Season with salt and black pepper and transfer to an immersion blender.
7. Pulse until smooth and refrigerate for about an hour before serving.

Nutrition Value: Calories: 187 Carbs: 9.4g Fats: 15.8g Proteins: 4.3g Sodium: 115mg Sugar: 4.4g

80. Chilled Cucumber Soup

Servings: 8

Preparation time: 15mins

Ingredients

- 3 large cucumbers, chopped
- 2 medium avocados, halved
- 2 cloves garlic, minced
- 2 large spring onions, roughly chopped
- 1 bunch fresh basil
- 3 tablespoons fresh lime juiceorlemon juice
- 2 cups water, vegetable stockor chicken stock
- ¾ teaspoon sea salt
- ¼ teaspoon black pepper, or to taste
- ½ cup extra virgin olive oil, divided
- 1 medium cucumber, thinly sliced

Directions

1. Put the cucumbers, avocados, onions, water, garlic, olive oil, basil, lime juice, salt and black pepper in an immersion blender.
2. Pulse until smooth and pour into a container.
3. Refrigerate for about 2 hours before serving.
4. Pour into serving bowls and top with the sliced cucumber.

Nutrition Value: Calories: 203 Carbs: 8.7g Fats: 19.6g Proteins: 1.9g Sodium: 374mg Sugar: 2.4g

81. Chilled Guacamole Soup

Servings: 6
Preparation time: 10 mins

Ingredients

- 2 avocados, peeled and pitted
- ¼ cup red onion, chopped

- 1 tablespoon fresh cilantro, chopped
- ¼ teaspoon black pepper
- ¼ cup whipping cream
- 2½ cups low-sodium chicken broth, divided
- 6 tablespoons cheddar cheese, shredded
- 2 garlic cloves, coarsely chopped
- 1 jalapeno, seeded and coarsely chopped
- 1 tablespoon lime juice
- ½ teaspoon salt
- ¼ teaspoon cayenne
- 2 tablespoons sour cream

Directions

1. Put 1 cup of chicken broth, garlic, jalapeño, avocados, lime juice, cilantro and onions in a food processor.
2. Pulse until smooth and add remaining broth, cayenne salt and black pepper.
3. Puree until smooth and transfer to a large bowl.
4. Stir in whipping cream and chill for at least 1 hour before serving.
5. Ladle into bowls and top with sour cream and shredded cheese.

Nutrition Value: Calories: 188 Carbs: 7.7g Fats: 15.3g Proteins: 6g Sodium: 317mg Sugar: 0.6g

82. Spinach Mint Soup with Sumac

Servings: 3
Preparation time: 10 mins

Ingredients

- 350gspinach leaves
- 400mlchicken stock
- ½ cup mint leaves

- 4spring onions,chopped
- 4 tablespoons heavy cream
- Pinch of sumac
- 1 tablespoon olive oil
- 2garlic cloves
- Salt and black pepper, to taste

Directions
1. Heat oil in a pot and add spring onions and garlic.
2. Sauté for about 3 minutes and add spinach leaves.
3. Cook for about 4 minutes and add chicken stock and mint leaves.
4. Transfer into a blender and blend until smooth.
5. Stir in heavy cream, salt, black pepper and a pinch of sumac.
6. Refrigerate and serve chilled.

Nutrition Value: Calories: 157 Carbs: 8.6g Fats: 13g Proteins: 5.1g Sodium: 538mg Sugar: 1.4g

83. Vegan Gazpacho

Servings: 6
Preparation time: 10 mins

Ingredients
- ½ red onion, finely chopped
- 2 tomatoes, finely chopped
- ½ medium cucumber, finely chopped
- ½ green pepper, seeded and finely chopped
- 6 celery stalks, finely chopped
- 1 garlic clove, crushed
- 2 cups tomato juice
1. 3 cup extra virgin olive oil
2. ¼ cup white wine vinegar

3. ¼ cup fresh parsley, finely chopped
4. 1 scoop stevia
5. Salt and black pepper, to taste

Directions

1. Put all the ingredients into a blender and blend until smooth.
2. Refrigerate for about 3 hours and serve chilled.

Nutrition Value: Calories: 133 Carbs: 8.2g Fats: 11.4g Proteins: 1.6g Sodium: 237mg Sugar: 5.3g

84. Chilled Avocado Arugula Soup

Servings: 6

Preparation time: 10 mins

Ingredients

- 2 medium ripe hass avocados, diced
- 65 grams arugula
- 3 cup mint leaves, roughly chopped
- 1 teaspoon sea salt
- 1 lemon, juiced
- 1 scoop stevia
- 3 cup heavy cream
- 3 cups spring water, ice cold
- 1 tablespoon olive oil
- 3 tablespoons goat cheese, for topping

Directions

1. Put all the ingredients into a blender and blend until smooth.
2. Dish out into bowls and top with goat cheese.

Nutrition Value: Calories: 167 Carbs: 6.2g Fats: 15.5g Proteins: 3.2g Sodium: 341mg Sugar: 0.6g

85. Chilled Cantaloupe Soup

Servings: 4
Preparation time: 10 mins

Ingredients

- 1 cantaloupe, cut into chunks
- 3 tablespoons butter
- 3 cup plain, non fat Greek yogurt
- 1 tablespoon ginger, freshly grated
- 1 scoop stevia
- ¼ teaspoon nutmeg
- Pinch of kosher salt
- 3 tablespoons fresh basil leaves, for garnish

Directions

1. Put all the ingredients into food processor except basil and pulse until smooth.
2. Refrigerate at least 2 hours before serving.
3. Garnish with fresh basil leaves and serve.

Nutrition Value: Calories: 87 Carbs: 4.7g Fats: 6.9g Proteins: 2.1g Sodium: 92mg Sugar: 3.2g

86. Chilled Peach Soup with Fresh Goat Cheese

Servings: 4
Preparation time: 1 hour 20 mins

Ingredients

- 2 peaches, sliced and peeled
- ¼ cup seedless cucumber, finely diced and peeled
- ¼ cup yellow bell pepper, finely diced
- ¼ cup dried apricots, diced
- 2 scoops stevia
- 3 tablespoons fresh goat cheese, crumbled

- ¼ cup white balsamic vinegar
- 3 cup extra-virgin olive oil
- 1 large garlic clove
- Basil leaves, for garnish
- Salt and black pepper, to taste

Directions

1. In a bowl, toss the peaches, diced cucumber, yellow pepper and apricots. Add the honey, 3 tablespoons of goat cheese, 1
2. 4 cup of balsamic vinegar and 2 tablespoons of the olive oil. Stir in 1 1
3. 2 teaspoons of salt. Add the garlic. Cover and refrigerate overnight.
4. Discard the garlic. Transfer the contents of the bowl to a blender and puree. Add 1
5. 4 cup of water and puree until very smooth and creamy; add more water if the soup seems too thick. Season with salt and vinegar. Refrigerate the soup until very cold, about 1 hour.
6. Meanwhile, in a medium skillet, heat the remaining 1
7. 4 cup of olive oil. Add the diced bread and cook over moderate heat, stirring, until golden and crisp, about 2 minutes. Using a slotted spoon, transfer the croutons to paper towels and season with salt.
8. Pour the peach soup into shallow bowls and garnish with the sliced cucumber, sliced bell pepper, goat cheese, croutons and basil. Drizzle lightly with olive oil, season with black pepper and serve.

Nutrition Value: Calories: 169 Carbs: 26.5g Fats: 4.7g Proteins: 5.3g Sodium: 262mg Sugar: 2.7g

87. Asparagus Soup

Servings:6

Preparation time: 1 hour and 10 minutes

Ingredients:

- 3 tablespoons ghee
- 1 white onion, chopped
- 5 cloves garlic, crushed
- 4 cups chicken broth
- 1 cup ham, diced
- 2 lb. asparagus, sliced in half
- ½ teaspoon dried thyme
- Salt and pepper to taste

Preparation Time:

1. Select the sauté function in the Instant Pot.
2. Add the ghee.
3. Add the onion and cook for 5 minutes.
4. Add the garlic, broth and ham.
5. Simmer for 3 minutes.
6. Add the asparagus and thyme.
7. Secure the pot.
8. Choose soup setting.
9. Cook for 45 minutes.
10. Blend the mixture in a food processor.
11. Season with the salt and pepper.
12. Serving Suggestion: Garnish with low-carb croutons.

Tip: You can also use an immersion blender instead of a food processor.

Nutrition Value:

Calories160
Total Fat 13.4g
Saturated Fat 7.9g
Cholesterol 29mg
Sodium 807mg
Total Carbohydrate 6.9g

Dietary Fiber 4g
Total Sugars 4.1g
Protein 10.7g

88. Carrot Soup

Servings:4
Preparation time: 20 minutes

Ingredients:

- ½ onion, diced
- 1 clove garlic, minced
- 8 carrots, sliced into cubes
- 2 cups vegetable broth
- 15 oz. coconut milk
- Salt and pepper to taste

Preparation Time:

1. Press the sauté button in the Instant Pot.
2. Add the oil.
3. Sauté onion and garlic for 1-3 minutes.
4. Add the carrots, vegetable broth and coconut milk.
5. Season with the salt and pepper.
6. Seal the pot.
7. Choose manual mode.
8. Cook at high pressure for 8 minutes.
9. Release the pressure naturally.
10. Use an immersion blender to blend the soup until smooth.
11. Serving Suggestion: Serve this soup with coconut cream and top with chopped parsley.

Tip: You can also use a regular blender to blend the soup.

Nutrition Value:

Calories320

Total Fat 26g
Saturated Fat 22.7g
Cholesterol 0mg
Sodium 482mg
Total Carbohydrate 19.9g
Dietary Fiber 5.7g
Total Sugars 10.5g
Protein 6.1g
Potassium 796mg

89. Spring Keto Stew with Venison

Servings:2
Preparation time: 20 minutes
Cooking Time: 6 hours

Ingredients:

- 1 lb venison stew meat
- 2 cup purple cabbage, shredded
- 2 cup celery, sliced
- 2 cup bone broth

Directions:

1. Sauté cabbage and celery with olive oil and garlic in a skillet.
2. Add the venison and season with salt and pepper to taste. Stir until meat is browned.
3. Transfer everything into the crockpot. Add the cone broth.
4. Cover and cook on low for 6 hours.

Nutrition Value:

Calories: 310, Fat: 16 g, Net carbs: 5 g, Protein: 32 g

Serving suggestions: When cooked, add the asparagus for

extra flavor and greens. Serve with lime if desired.

90. Mexican Taco Soup

Servings:2
Preparation time: 5 minutes
Cooking Time: 4 hours

Ingredients:
- 1 lb ground meat, browned
- 8 oz cream cheese
- 10 oz diced tomatoes and chilis
- 1 tbsp of taco seasonings
- 1 cup of chicken broth

Directions:
- Combine all ingredients in the crockpot.
- Cook on low for 4 hours.

Nutrition Value:

Calories: 547, Fat: 43 g, Net carbs: 5 g, Protein: 33 g

Serving suggestions: Stir in cilantro or garnish with shredded cheese before serving.

91. Oxtail Stew

Servings:2
Preparation time: 20 minutes
Cooking Time: 10 hours

Ingredients:
- 2 lb oxtail, chopped
- 10 tomatoes, diced
- 4 tsp paprika

Directions:

1. Place oxtail in the crockpot with water filling up to half the pot.
2. Cover and cook for 10 hours on low.
3. When cooked, transfer the oxtail to a saucepan and add the tomatoes paprika and other desired seasonings (garlic cloves, chili powder, salt).
4. Stew for 15 minutes.

Nutrition Value:

Calories: 456, Fat: 29 g, Net carbs: 7 g, Protein: 37 g

92. Rabbit Stew

Servings:2
Preparation time: 20 minutes
Cooking Time: 6 hours

Ingredients:

- 1 rabbit, browned
- 1 lb andouille sausage, cut to 1
- 2 inches thick
- 3 medium carrots, 1-inch chunks
- 2 qt chicken stock
- Spices of choice

Directions:

1. Sauté onion, sausage and desired spices in a skillet, then add half of the stock to deglaze.
2. Put the rabbit in the crockpot and add the contents of the skillet.
3. Cover and cook for 6 hours on high.

Nutrition Value:

Calories: 381, Fat: 32 g, Net carbs: 4 g, Protein: 29 g

Tip: You can add mushrooms for extra flavor.

93. Rosemary Turkey and Kale Soup

Servings:2
Preparation time: 20 minutes
Cooking Time: 8 hours

Ingredients:
- 2 carrots, sliced
- 2 cups turkey stock
- 1 sprig rosemary
- 2 cups turkey meat, bite-size pieces
- 2 cups kale, chopped

Directions:
1. Sauté onion, carrots and desired spices in a skillet, then add half of the stock to deglaze.
2. Put the turkey in the crockpot and add the contents of the skillet.
3. Cover and cook for 8 hours on low.
4. Add the kale when cooked.

Nutrition Value:
Calories: 403, Fat: 28 g, Net carbs: 6 g, Protein: 34 g
Serving suggestions: Remove the turkey rosemary before serving.
Tip: If the soup is to be served later, do not add the kale until just before serving.

94. Ham Cauliflower Soup

Preparation time: 10 minutes
Cooking time: 60 minutes
Servings: 10

Nutrition Value:

Carbs –6 g
Net Carbs: 1.7 g
Fat: 20 g
Protein: 10 g
Calories: 246

Ingredients:

- 3 Tbsp olive oil
- ½ yellow onion, chopped
- 3 cloves garlic, sliced
- 1 leftover ham bone, with 2-3 cups ham still attached
- 4 cups low-sodium chicken broth1 medium head of cauliflower, cut into small florets
- 1 cup heavy cream
- 1 cup white cheddar, shredded
- Salt, pepper, to taste
- 1¼ cups sour cream
- ½ cup green onions, sliced (optional)

Directions:

1. Turn Instant Pot on to "Sauté" setting. Add olive oil. When olive oil is hot, stir in onions and garlic. Season with salt and pepper. Cook for 2 minutes or until garlic is fragrant.
2. Add in ham bone and broth. Turn off heat. Put on lid and set valve to sealing. Cook on high pressure for 50 minutes.
3. Quick release pressure and allow the button to drop on lid. Remove ham bone and cut the meat off the bone. Chop the ham and return it to the pot.
4. Add cauliflower florets and heavy cream. Season soup with salt and pepper; stir. Put on lid, set the valve sealing, and cook on high pressure for 5 more minutes.
5. Quick release pressure and allow the button to drop on lid. Stir in cheese and ladle soup into bowls. Top

each bowl with 2 Tbsp sour cream and a few green onions.

95. Spicy Pork & Spinach Stew

Preparation time: 10 minutes
Cooking time: 30 minutes
Servings: 6

Nutrition Value:

Carbs: 9 g
Net Carbs: 3.7 g
Fat: 17 g
Protein: 23 g
Calories: 291

Ingredients:

- 1 large onion
- 4 cloves garlic
- 10 oz Rotel
- 1 tsp dried thyme
- 2 tsp Tony Chachere seasoning
- 1 pound pork butt, cut into 2-inch chunks
- ½ cup heavy whipping cream
- 4-6 cups baby spinach, chopped

Directions:

1. Mix together onion, garlic, and Rotel.
2. Pour the mixture into the Instant Pot. Mix in the pork cubes and Tony Chachere seasoning.
3. Turn on Instant Pot, press the "Meat" button, adjust the timer for 20 minutes. Let the pressure to release naturally for 10 minutes and then release any remaining pressure.
4. Turn the Instant Pot to "Sauté." Once stew begins to boil, add the cream and stir well.

5. Add spinach leaves and cook until wilted. Serve.

96. Smothered Pork Chops

Preparation time: 10 minutes
Cooking time: 40 minutes
Servings: 7

Nutrition Value:
Carbs: 6.73 g
Net Carbs: 4.06 g
Fat: 32 g
Protein: 40 g
Calories: 481

Ingredients:
- 1 tsp garlic powder
- 1 tsp onion powder
- 1 tsp black pepper
- 1 tsp salt
- ¼ tsp cayenne pepper
- 1 Tbsp paprika
- 4 4-6-ounce pork loin chops, boneless
- 2 tsp coconut oil
- ½ medium onion, sliced
- 6 ounces sliced baby Bella mushrooms
- 1 tsp butter
- ½ cup heavy cream
- ½ tsp xanthan gum
- 1 Tbsp chopped fresh parsley

Directions:
1. In a small bowl, mix the first six ingredients.
2. Rinse and pat dry the pork chops.
3. Rub the pork chops with 1 Tbsp of the spice mixture

each. Reserve the remaining spices.

4. Add the coconut oil to the Instant Pot and press "Sauté." Heat for 2 minutes

5. Add the pork chops to the coconut oil and brown for 3 minutes per side. Remove the pork chops and turn off the Instant Pot.

6. Add the browned pork, onions, and mushrooms to pot base.

7. Cover the Instant Pot with lid and make sure the vent is sealed. Cook on the Manual High setting for 25 minutes. Once time is up, let the pressure release naturally.

8. Uncover and place just the pork chops on a serving plate.

9. Press "Sauté" again and whisk in the remaining spice mixture, butter, xanthan gum, and heavy cream into the hot liquid.

10. Let the gravy simmer for 3-5 minutes. Turn off the Pot.

11. Top the pork chops with the mushroom gravy and onion. Garnish with parsley and serve.

97. Creamy Garlic Mushroom Chicken Stew

Preparation time: 15 minutes
Cooking time: 25 minutes
Servings: 4

Nutrition Value:

Carbs: 5.6 g
Net Carbs: 3 g
Fat: 17 g
Protein: 18 g
Calories: 189

Ingredients:

- 1 brown onion, sliced

- 2 Tbsp olive oil
- 1 tsp salt
- 1.7 lbs chicken thighs or breast, diced
- 7 oz mix of Swiss brown & white button mushrooms
- 4 large garlic cloves, diced
- 1-2 bay leaves
- ¼ tsp nutmeg powder
- ½ tsp black pepper
- ½ cup chicken stock
- 1 tsp Dijon mustard
- 3 cup sour cream
- 1 tsp arrowroot, cornstarch, or tapioca starch for thickening
- 2-3 Tbsp parsley, chopped

Directions:
1. Turn the Instant Pot on and press the "Sauté" function key.
2. Combine the onion, olive oil, and salt in the pot. Cook for 3-4 minutes, until soft.
3. Add the next eight ingredients and stir thoroughly.
4. Press "Keep Warm
5. Cancel." Put on and lock the lid, the steam releasing handle should point to Sealing.
6. Press "Poultry" (High Pressure) for 15 minutes. After 3 beeps the pressure cooker will start. Let the pressure release naturally for 5 minutes, then use the quick release to let off the rest of the steam.
7. Uncover and press the "Sauté" function key again. Scoop out a few tablespoons of the liquid and dissolve in the arrowroot in it. Pour the mixture back into the pot and stir.
8. Stir in the sour cream. Press "Keep Warm
9. Cancel" to stop the cooking process.

10. Top with chopped parsley and serve.

98. Garlic Butter Chicken

Preparation time: 5 minutes
Cooking time: 40 minutes
Servings: 4

Nutrition Value:
Carbs: 3 g
Net Carbs: 1.4 g
Fat: 21 g
Protein: 47 g
Calories: 404

Ingredients:
- 4 chicken breasts, chopped
- ¼ cup turmeric ghee (+ more for serving)
- 1 tsp salt (add more to taste)
- 10 cloves garlic, peeled, diced

Directions:
1. Put the chicken breasts into the Instant Pot. Then stir in the ghee, salt, and diced garlic.
2. Set the Instant Pot on high pressure for 35 minutes. Let the pressure to release naturally for 10 minutes and then release any remaining pressure. Unlock and remove the lid.
3. Shred the chicken breast in the pot.
4. Serve with additional ghee and salt if needed.

99. Keto Creamy Chicken Bacon Chowder

Preparation time: 8-10 minutes (+8 hours)
Cooking time: 30 minutes
Servings: 4-6

Nutrition Value:

Carbs: 7 g
Net Carbs: 3.4 g
Fat: 25 g
Protein: 25 g
Calories: 365

Ingredients:

- 6 chicken thighs, boneless
- 8 oz cream cheese, full fat
- 4 tsp minced garlic
- ½ cup celery
- ½ frozen onion, chopped
- 6 oz mushrooms, sliced
- 4 Tbsp butter
- 1 tsp thyme
- Salt, pepper, to taste
- 3 cups chicken broth
- 1 cup heavy cream
- 1 lb cooked bacon, chopped
- 2 cups fresh spinach

Directions:

1. Cube chicken thighs and put inside Ziploc bag.
2. Add remaining ingredients to bag and seal. Refrigerate for 8 hours.
3. Pour chicken mixture into Instant Pot, add chicken broth and cook for 30 minutes on "Soup" setting.
4. Mix well, then stir in spinach and cream. Cover and let sit for 10 minutes to wilt the spinach. Top with chopped bacon.
5. Serve warm.

100. Buffalo Chicken Soup

Preparation time: 10 minutes
Cooking time: 20 minutes
Servings: 6

Nutrition Value:

Carbs: 4 g
Net Carbs: 2.6 g
Fat: 16 g
Protein: 27 g
Calories: 270

Ingredients:

- 1 Tbsp extra-virgin olive oil
- ½ large onion, diced
- ½ cup celery, diced
- 4 cloves garlic, minced
- 1 lb chicken, cooked, shredded
- 4 cup chicken bone broth
- 3 Tbsp Buffalo sauce
- 6 oz cream cheese, cubed, at room temperature
- ½ cup heavy cream

Directions:

1. Press "Saute" button on the Instant Pot. Add the oil, chopped onion, and celery. Cook for 5-10 minutes, until onions are translucent and start to brown.
2. Add garlic. Saute for a minute, until fragrant. Press the "Off" button.
3. Add the shredded chicken, broth, and buffalo sauce.
4. Cover and seal the Instant Pot. Press the "Soup" button and adjust the time to 5 minutes. After the time is up, allow the natural pressure release for 5 minutes, then switch to quick release and open the lid.
5. Ladle about a cup of liquid from the edge of the Instant Pot and put in blender. Add cream cheese and puree

until smooth.

6. Add the mixture back into the Instant Pot with the heavy cream. Stir until smooth.

101. Creamy Mushroom Chicken Stew

Preparation time: 15 minutes
Cooking time: 25 minutes
Servings: 4

Nutrition Value:

Carbs: 5.6 g
Net Carbs: 3 g
Fat: 17 g
Protein: 18 g
Calories: 189

Ingredients:

- 1 brown onion, sliced
- 2 Tbsp olive oil
- 1 tsp salt
- 1.7 lbs chicken thighs or breast, diced
- 7 oz mix of Swiss brown & white button mushrooms
- 4 large garlic cloves, diced
- 1-2 bay leaves
- ¼ tsp nutmeg powder
- ½ tsp black pepper
- ½ cup chicken stock
- 1 tsp Dijon mustard
- 3 cup sour cream
- 1 tsp arrowroot, cornstarch, or tapioca starch for thickening
- 2-3 Tbsp parsley, chopped

Directions:

1. Turn the Instant Pot on and press the "Sauté" function key.
2. Combine the onion, olive oil, and salt in the pot. Cook for 3-4 minutes, until soft.
3. Add the next eight ingredients and stir thoroughly.
4. Press "Keep Warm
5. Cancel." Put on and lock the lid, the steam releasing handle should point to Sealing.
6. Press "Poultry" (High Pressure) for 15 minutes. After 3 beeps the pressure cooker will start. Let the pressure release naturally for 5 minutes, then use the quick release to let off the rest of the steam.
7. Uncover and press the "Sauté" function key again. Scoop out a few tablespoons of the liquid and dissolve in the arrowroot in it. Pour the mixture back into the pot and stir.
8. Stir in the sour cream. Press "Keep Warm
9. Cancel" to stop the cooking process.
10. Top with chopped parsley and serve.

102. Taco Soup

Preparation time: 10 minutes
Cooking time: 10 minutes
Servings: 8

Nutrition Value:

Carbs: 8 g
Net Carbs: 3.7 g
Fat: 28 g
Protein: 27 g
Calories: 368

Ingredients:
- 2 lbs ground beef
- 1 Tbsp onion flakes

- 4 cloves garlic, minced
- 2 Tbsp chili powder
- 2 tsp cumin
- 20 oz tomatoes with chilis, diced
- 32 oz beef broth
- Salt, pepper, to taste
- 8 oz cream cheese
- ½ cup heavy cream

Directions:

1. Press the "Sauté" button, brown ground beef in the Instant Pot. Drain excess grease if needed.
2. Stir in the next seven ingredients. Cover Instant Pot and cook on "Soup" setting for 5 minutes.
3. When time is up, allow the pot to sit with the valve closed to depressurize for 1 minute before opening vent valve and removing the lid. Add cream cheese and heavy cream.
4. Serve hot.

103. Chicken Mushroom Soup

Preparation time: 5 minutes
Cooking time:20 minutes
Servings: 4

Nutrition Value:

Carbs: 9 g
Net Carbs: 3.2 g
Fat: 15 g
Protein: 30 g
Calories: 289

Ingredients:

- 1 onion, sliced

- 3 cloves garlic, minced
- 2 cups mushrooms. chopped
- 1 yellow squash chopped
- 1 lb chicken breast, boneless, skinless, cut into large chunks
- 2½ cups chicken stock
- Salt, pepper, to taste
- 1 tsp Italian seasoning or poultry seasoning
- ½ cup heavy whipping cream, optional

Directions:
1. Put all ingredients into the inner liner of the Instant Pot.
2. Cover the Instant Pot with a lid and set it to cook at high pressure for 5 minutes. Let natural pressure release for 10 minutes, then release all remaining pressure.
3. Take out chicken pieces and let chill.
4. Purée the vegetables and liquid in a blender, then return to Instant Pot.
5. Shred the chicken and add to liquid. Stir in heavy whipping cream if using. Mix well. Serve warm.

104. Thai Green Curry

Preparation time: 15 minutes
Cooking time: 8 hours
Servings: 6

Nutrition Value:

Carbs: 5 g
Net Carbs: 2.3 g
Fat: 18 g
Protein: 15 g
Calories: 241

Ingredients:

- 1 Tbsp coconut oil
- 2 Tbsp curry paste
- 1 Tbsp ginger, minced
- 1 Tbsp garlic
- ½ cup onion, sliced
- 1 lb boneless, skinless chicken thighs
- 2 cups chopped, peeled eggplant
- 1 chopped green-yellow, or orange pepper
- ½ cup Thai basil leaves
- 1 cup unsweetened coconut milk
- 1 Tbsp fish sauce
- 2 Tbsp soy sauce
- 2 tsp Splenda
- 1 tsp salt

Directions:

1. Turn your Instant Pot on "Sauté" on high. Add coconut oil. Once the oil is hot, add the curry paste and cook for 1-2 minutes.
2. Stir in ginger and garlic and cook for 30 seconds. Add the onions and stir thoroughly.
3. Stir in all remaining ingredients and deglaze the bottom of the pan.
4. Press "Cancel" to turn off the "Sauté" setting and press "Slow Cook" button. Adjust the time to 8 hours.
5. Serve warm.

105. Cauliflower Soup

Preparation time: 5 minutes
Cooking time: 40 minutes
Servings: 4

Nutrition Value:

Carbs: 3 g

Net Carbs: 1.4 g

Fat: 21 g

Protein: 47 g

Calories: 404

Ingredients:

- 1 Tbsp olive oil
- 1 large yellow onion, diced
- 2 cloves garlic, minced
- 1 head cauliflower, coarsely chopped
- 1 green bell pepper, chopped
- 1 Tbsp onion powder
- Salt, ground black pepper, to taste
- 32 oz chicken stock
- 2 cups cheddar cheese, shredded
- 1 cup half and half
- 6 slices turkey bacon, cooked, diced
- 1 Tbsp Dijon mustard
- 4 dashes hot pepper sauce

Directions:

1. Turn on Instant Pot and press "Sauté" button.
2. Add olive oil, onion, and garlic. Cook for about 3 minutes to brown.
3. Stir in cauliflower, green bell pepper, onion powder, salt, and pepper.
4. Pour in chicken stock, then close and lock the lid.
5. Select "Soup" function and adjust the time to 35 minutes.
6. Let the pressure release naturally for 10 minutes and then release any remaining pressure. Unlock and remove the lid.
7. Stir in the remaining ingredients.

8. Reselect "Sauté" function, and cook for about 5 minutes until bubbly.
9. Serve warm.

106. Keto Low Carb Chili

Preparation time: 15 minutes
Cooking time: 1 hour
Servings: 10

Nutrition Value:
Carbs: 13 g
Net Carbs: 10 g
Fat: 18 g
Protein: 23 g
Calories: 306

Ingredients:
- 2 ½ lbs ground beef
- ½ large onion, chopped
- 8 cloves garlic, minced
- 2 15-oz can diced tomatoes, with liquid
- 1 6-oz can tomato paste
- 1 4-oz can green chiles, with liquid
- 2 Tbsp Worcestershire sauce
- ¼ cup chili powder
- 2 Tbsp cumin
- 1 Tbsp dried oregano
- 2 tsp sea salt
- 1 tsp black pepper
- 1 medium bay leaf
- 1 cup water

Directions:
1. Select the Sauté setting on your Instant Pot. Cook the

chopped onion and for 5-7 minutes, then add the garlic and cook for one minute, until fragrant.
2. Stir in the ground beef. Cook for 8-10 minutes, until browned.
3. Add remaining ingredients, except bay leaf, to the Instant Pot and stir until combined. Add a cup of water.
4. Close the lid. Press "Keep Warm
5. Cancel" to stop the saute cycle. Select the "Meat
6. Stew" setting (35 minutes) to start pressure cooking.
7. Serve warm.

107. Tomatillo Chili

Preparation time: 15 minutes
Cooking time: 40 minutes
Servings: 8

Nutrition Value:

Carbs: 6 g
Net Carbs: 5 g
Fat: 23 g
Protein: 20 g
Calories: 325

Ingredients:

- 1 lb ground beef
- 1 lb ground pork
- 3 tomatillos, chopped
- ½ white onion, chopped
- 6 oz tomato paste
- 1 tsp garlic powder
- 1 jalapeno pepper, chopped, including seeds
- 1 Tbsp ground cumin
- 1 Tbsp chili powder

- Salt, to taste

Directions:
1. Turn the Instant Pot on and press "Sauté." Brown the beef and pork in the Instant Pot for 5-7 minutes.
2. Mix in the remaining ingredients.
3. Cover and lock the pressure cooker. Cook at high pressure for 35 minutes, then turn off and allow the pressure release naturally.
4. Serve with your favorite low carb toppings!

108. White Chicken Chili

Preparation time: 20 minutes
Cooking time: 1 hour
Servings: 8

Nutrition Value:
Carbs: 12 g
Net Carbs: 8.5 g
Fat: 33 g
Protein: 41 g
Calories: 509

Ingredients:
- 2 Tbsp butter
- 1 medium onion, diced
- 10 medium chicken thighs, boneless, skinless, cubed
- 1 14-oz can green chiles, diced
- 2 tsp salt
- 2 tsp cumin
- 2 tsp oregano
- 1 tsp black pepper
- 1 lb frozen cauliflower
- 4 cups chicken broth

- 2 cups sour cream
- 1 cup heavy whipping cream

Directions:
1. Turn the Instant Pot on and press the "Sauté" function key. Melt the butter.
2. Add the onion and chicken. Cook for 10 minutes, until the chicken browned
3. Stir in the green chiles, salt, cumin, oregano, black pepper, and frozen cauliflower.
4. Pour in the chicken broth. Cover and lock the instant pot, cooking on high pressure for 30 minutes.
5. Set aside for 10 minutes. Let the natural pressure release for 10 minutes.
6. Whisk in the sour cream and heavy whipping cream. Serve immediately.

109. Black Bean & Lentil Chilli
Preparation time: 5 minutes
Cooking time: 15 minutes
Servings: 6

Nutrition Value:
Carbs: 5 g
Net Carbs: 4 g
Fat: 2 g
Protein: 8 g
Calories: 144

Ingredients:
- 1 Tbsp olive oil
- 2 chopped carrots
- 1 Tbsp paprika
- 1 Tbsp dried oregano
- 2 tsp garlic powder

- 2 tsp cumin
- 1 ounce dried mushrooms
- 1 cup lentils
- 2 cups dry black beans
- 114 ounce can of chopped tomatoes
- 4 cups of water
- 2 Tbsp Worcestershire sauce
- 1 teaspoon salt

Directions:
1. Preheat your pressure cooker using a 'sauté' or 'brown' program.
2. Chop the onions and the carrot.
3. Add the oil and onion to the pressure cooker.
4. Add the spices, mushrooms, carrots and tomatoes, mix well.
5. Close the lid and set the pressure cooker valve for 10 minutes on high.
6. Add the salt.
7. Add the Worcestershire sauce and combine.
8. Serve in a bowl.

110. Salsa Verde Chicken Soup

Preparation time: 10 minutes
Cooking time: 45 minutes
Servings: 4

Nutrition Value:
Carbs: 8.6 g
Net Carbs: 6.7 g
Fat: 18.3 g
Protein: 33.5 g
Calories: 340

Ingredients:

- 4 chicken breasts, on the bone, skin intact (about 1½ pounds)
- ½ tsp salt
- ½ tsp mild chili powder
- ¼ tsp freshly ground black pepper
- 2 Tbsp olive oil
- ½ red or white onion, minced
- 2 cups cauliflower florets
- 2 cups fresh cilantro leaves and stems, chopped and divided
- 4 garlic cloves
- 1 quart unsalted chicken broth
- ½ cup commercial salsa verde
- ¼ cup sour cream

Directions:

1. Sprinkle the chicken with the salt, chili powder, and pepper. Warm the oil in a stockpot over medium heat. Add the chicken and cook for 8 minutes, turning

2. a few times, until the chicken is well browned. Transfer the chicken to a plate.Add the onion, cauliflower, half the cilantro, and the garlic, cooking 5 to 6 minutes more, until the vegetables soften.

3. Return the chicken to the stockpot, and cover with the broth. Bring to a simmer and cook 20 to 25 minutes, until the chicken is cooked through. Remove the skin and bones. Shred the chicken. Return it to the soup, and top with the salsa verde and the remaining cilantro. Serve with the sour cream.

111. Cauliflower & Cheddar Soup

Preparation time: 10 minutes
Cooking time: 30 minutes

Servings: 8

Nutrition Value:

Carbs: 4 g
Net Carbs: 2 g
Fat: 21 g
Protein: 8 g
Calories: 227

Ingredients:

- ¼ cup butter
- ½ sweet onion, chopped
- 1 head cauliflower, chopped
- 4 cups chicken stock
- ½ tsp ground nutmeg
- 1 cup heavy (whipping) cream
- Sea salt, black pepper, to taste
- 1 cup Cheddar cheese, shredded

Directions:

1. In a stockpot, melt the butter.
2. Sauté the onion and cauliflower for 10 minutes.
3. Stir in the chicken stock and nutmeg and bring it to a boil. Then simmer for 15 minutes.
4. Add the heavy cream, and purée the soup with a food processor until smooth.
5. Season with salt and pepper and top with Cheddar cheese. Serve.

112. Lemon Butter Chicken

Preparation time: 10 minutes
Cooking time: 40 minutes
Servings: 4

Nutrition Value:

Carbs: 4 g
Net Carbs: 3 g
Fat: 26 g
Protein: 12 g
Calories: 294

Ingredients:

- 4 chicken thighs, bone-in, skin-on
- Sea salt, black pepper, to taste
- 2 Tbsp butter, divided
- 2 tsp garlic, minced
- ½ cup chicken stock
- ½ cup heavy (whipping) cream
- Juice of ½ lemon

Directions:

1. Preheat the oven to 400°F.
2. Place an ovenproof skillet and add 1 Tbsp of butter. Season the chicken thighs with salt and pepper.
3. Brown the chicken thighs for about 6 minutes in total. Remove the thighs to a plate and set aside.
4. Add the remaining 1 Tbsp of butter and sauté the garlic until translucent, about 2 minutes.
5. Mix in the chicken stock, heavy cream, and lemon juice.
6. Bring the sauce to a boil and then return the chicken to the skillet.
7. Place the skillet in the oven, covered, and braise until the chicken is cooked through, about 30 minutes.

113. Chicken Vegetable Soup

Preparation time: 15 minutes
Cooking time: 1 hour 20 minutes
Servings: 3

Nutrition Value:

Carbs: 6 g
Net Carbs: 5.5 g
Fat: 12.8 g
Protein: 33.2 g
Calories: 189

Ingredients:

- 1 pound skinless chicken breasts
- ½ cup chopped carrots
- ¼ cup chopped celery
- ¼ cup chopped onion
- Salt and pepper

Directions:

1. Cook chicken breasts in a pot with 2½ cups of water over medium heat for 20 minutes.
2. Remove the chicken from the broth and cut into strips.
3. Put the chicken strips back into the pot with the broth.
4. Season with salt and pepper.
5. Add the rest of the ingredients.
6. Cook for about 1 hour more or until vegetables are done.

114. Beef Bourguignon

Preparation time: 30 minutes
Cooking time: 3 hours
Servings: 4

Nutrition Value:

Carbs: 8.9 g
Net Carbs: 7.2 g
Fat: 30.3 g
Protein: 28.2 g

Calories: 461

Ingredients:
- 1 pound beef stew meat
- 1 Tbsp flour mix
- ½ tsp salt
- ¼ tsp freshly ground black pepper
- 2 Tbsp unsalted butter
- 2 Tbsp olive oil
- ¼ pound bacon, chopped
- 10 ounces mushrooms, such as cremini, trimmed and sliced
- ½ onion, chopped
- 4 garlic cloves, minced
- 2 Tbsp tomato paste
- 1 tsp fresh thyme leaves
- 1 cup dry red wine
- 2 cups beef broth

Directions:
1. Put the beef on a plate, and sprinkle with the flour mix, salt, and pepper. Toss to coat evenly. Set aside.
2. Warm the butter and olive oil in a large stockpot or Dutch oven over medium-high heat. Add the beef and cook 4 to 5 minutes, turning occasionally, until the coating browns. Transfer the beef to a plate.
3. Add in the bacon and cook for 5 minutes, stirring often, scraping up any brown bits that stick to the inside of the pot. Add the mushrooms, onion, and garlic; cook 4 to 5 minutes, stirring often, until the mushrooms soften and the onion is brown. Then reduce the heat to low, and add the tomato paste and thyme, cooking 1 minute more, until the tomato paste is fragrant.Pour in the red wine and broth, and increase the heat to high. Return the beef to the pot,

and bring to a boil, then immediately reduce to a simmer and cover. Cook for 3 hours, until the beef is tender and the sauce thickens. Serve immediately.

115. Beef Arrabiata Ragu

Preparation time: 15 minutes
Cooking time: 15 minutes
Servings: 4

Nutrition Value:

Carbs: 10.9 g
Net Carbs: 7.6 g
Fat: 40.2 g
Protein: 24.8 g
Calories: 500

Ingredients:

- 4 medium zucchini, spiralized
- ½ tsp salt
- 2 Tbsp ghee or lard, divided
- 2 cloves garlic, minced
- 1 pound ground beef
- 1 cup unsweetened canned tomatoes
- 2 Tbsp unsweetened tomato paste
- ¼ cup water or bone broth
- 1 tsp red pepper flakes
- 2 tsp dried Italian herb mix
- Salt and pepper
- 2 Tbsp extra-virgin olive oil
- Fresh basil
- ½ cup (45 g
- 1.6 oz) grated Parmesan cheese

Directions:

1. Sprinkle the spiralized zucchini "noodles" with salt and let them sit for 10 minutes. Pat them dry. Set aside.
2. Grease a large pan with 1 Tbsp of the ghee and place over medium-high heat. Add the garlic and cook for about 1 minute, until fragrant.
3. Add the beef and cook for 5 minutes. Add the tomatoes, tomato paste, water, red pepper flakes, Italian herb mix, and salt and pepper to taste. Cook for about 3 to 5 more minutes, then remove from the heat.
4. Grease another pan with the remaining 1 Tbsp ghee. Cook the zucchini noodles for 2 to 5 minutes, tossing them in the pan while cooking.
5. Serve the noodles topped with the prepared ragu, drizzled with the olive oil, and garnished with fresh basil. Sprinkle with grated Parmesan cheese.

116. Salted Caramel Pork Rinds

Preparation time: 40 minutes
Cooking time: 15 minutes
Servings: 4

Nutrition Value:
Carbs: 2.6 g
Net Carbs: 2 g
Fat: 46 g
Protein: 14 g
Calories: 510

Ingredients:
- 1 oz pork rinds
- 1 cup unsweetened vanilla coconut milk
- 2 Tbsp heavy cream
- 2 Tbsp butter
- 1 Tbsp erythritol

Directions:

1. Add butter to the pan over medium heat. Remove from heat and add erythritol and heavy cream. Mix well and return heat.
2. Allow the caramel mixture to bubble.
3. Stir in pork rinds.
4. Transfer pork rinds to a container and place in the fridge for 30 minutes.
5. Serve with milk and enjoy!

CONCLUSION

Remember that like any other diet plans; Ketogenic has negative or adverse effects too. Make sure to consult your doctor first before implementing this diet strategy. This kind of diet is quite strict and requires a lot of willpower to avoid sugary-laden, high-caloric foods, or drinks. It needs a lot of discipline to stick to this diet, especially during the first few days or weeks because of metabolic shift. But remember to adhere to the rules to avoid common dieting pitfalls. Let the transition occurs naturally and smoothly. The reward at the end is beneficial to your overall wellbeing.

Manufactured by
Amazon.ca
Bolton, ON